HELD FAST IN HIS ARMS

(Learning to Trust God)

by

Kathryn Master Pendergrass

Held Fast In His Arms
(Learning to Trust God)
by Kathryn Master Pendergrass

Printed in the United States of America.

ISBN 9781498443838

www.xulonpress.com

TABLE OF CONTENTS

INTRODUCTION

Sometimes we go through very hard things. Sometimes the road is easy, and the days are filled with joy, but sometimes the way is hard, and the days are filled with pain. God is with us always! However, it seems our hearts search Him out and are more open to receiving Him when we are lost and confused, or wondering "Why, God, why?"

I wrote this book to share with you my own life journey and how Jesus has carried me through it all. It is a joy to tell you about the wonderful things He has done for me! It is my hope that these stories will encourage you and deepen your faith and certainty in God's love and care for you. I pray that these descriptions of true events in my own life will:

1) strengthen your faith, if you are in doubt;
2) lift up your spirits if you are in a period of discouragement;
3) renew your joy in His love if you are going through tough circumstances; and, finally and most importantly,
4) draw you closer to Him.

I know these things with certainty, deep down in my spirit:

1) Jesus is *always* good, *always* loving.
2) Jesus will love me forever, and my love for Him will only grow richer and deeper as I walk with Him and grow

closer to Him. His love is far greater than my human mind can even comprehend or imagine. I can <u>never</u> lose His love!

3) Jesus will be with me and I will be with Him now and forevermore.

4) **Jesus never fails me**. He will **never** lead me on a wrong path. I can trust Him **in all**!

5) Jesus knows the beginning and the end of my life (and of all creation). He is the Alpha and the Omega.

These are certainties not only for me, but for all who will receive Him as Lord and Savior. **He welcomes us into His arms, to be held fast in His love**. May God's blessings rest upon you as you read this little book, dedicated to Him.

DEDICATION

Psalm 121

¹ I lift up my eyes to the mountains—
where does my help come from?
² My help comes from the LORD,
the Maker of heaven and earth.
³ He will not let your foot slip—
he who watches over you will not slumber;
⁴ indeed, he who watches over Israel
will neither slumber nor sleep.
⁵ The LORD watches over you—
the LORD is your shade at your right hand,
⁶ the sun will not harm you by day,
nor the moon by night.
⁷ The LORD will keep you from all harm—
he will watch over your life;
⁸ the LORD will watch over your coming and going
both now and forevermore.

ACKNOWLEDGEMENTS

$\mathcal{I}$ want to thank all the friends and family who have helped me and given me encouragement in writing this book. My deepest gratitude to my husband, Daniel, whose love, honesty and support have been a constant source of strength and comfort. Heartfelt thanks and appreciation for all my dear family, with special thanks to my nieces Kate Holzer and Leslie Prevish, nephews Tom and Dave Prevish, my sister Sue Beichner, my brother Jack Master and my sister-in-law Debbie Master for their constant love and support. A special thank you to my longtime friends Maureen Farrell, Ellen Pearl and Bill Anderson for their loving support through the years. Thank you also to all of the many friends and relatives who have supported me in this project, among them: Phil Bliss, Ria Carlo, Kim Eck, Sharon Flowers, Karen Fugate, Rich and Cindy Hart, Michael Green, Dale Hastings, Lois Johnson, Reyn and Doris Kamphius, Kim Mossel, Harry Murchison, Cathie Myer, Janet Poles, Howard Roshaven, Rosemary Seto, Estelle Schultz, Jane Foard Thompson, and Kay Westendorf.

Additionally, thank you to the many Christian brothers and sisters both presently in my life and in the past who have prayed for me, encouraged me, and have shown me Christ's love in their living examples. I am inspired and in awe of all of you--your examples of love and strength have lifted me up many times! Special mention to Fran Dial, who prayed with me and led me to a personal relationship with Jesus Christ in 1979, and Maaike Callan and Adrienne May for their faithful prayers. Thank you also to my present church family at St. Mary Magdalene Church, Lakewood Ranch, Florida. Finally and most gratefully, thanks and praise to Him to whom I owe EVERYTHING: Jesus Christ, my Lord and Savior.

PART I:
HELD FAST IN HIS ARMS

CHAPTER ONE

GOD IS OMNIPOTENT: EVERYTHING IS IN HIS HANDS

(There is _nothing_ outside of His control. There are no exceptions to this.)

"For you created my inmost being; you knit me together in my mother's womb. I praise you because I am fearfully and wonderfully made; your works are wonderful, I know that full well. My frame was not hidden from you when I was made in the secret place, when I was woven together in the depths of the earth. Your eyes saw my unformed body; all the days ordained for me were written in your book before one of them came to be." (Psalm 139:13-16)

I was so afraid. Would I lose this baby too? I was eight weeks along in my second pregnancy and now I was bleeding heavily. I had waited so long for this baby and wanted it so much! My first child had died at age two months of a brain tumor. When I learned I was pregnant again, I was so excited and happy. I could not bear the thought of losing another child!

My husband and I had moved to Philadelphia three years ago, finally ready to start a family, after five years of marriage. We had met at West Virginia University in our freshman year of college.

"David" (not his real name) played the oboe, and I played the flute in our college band. We both sat in the first row, which was laid out in a half-circle pattern. I sat on the far right end playing flute, and he was in the middle as an oboist, with five people sitting between us. A "chatterbox", I was often laughing and talking to the players next to me during rehearsal, and David would look over and raise one eyebrow quizzically (which always intrigued me--I could not raise just one eyebrow at a time!). David was tall and very thin, with dark curly hair, a high forehead, and blue eyes set wide apart that measured his world with sober intelligence. I was 5'4", blue-eyed and fair-skinned, exuberant, rarely sitting still for long.

One day it was raining when we came out of band practice. David offered me the protection of his umbrella and walked with me back to my dorm. David was a chemistry major, extremely smart (Mensa material), cautious and always thinking ahead, so naturally he was prepared for the sudden rainstorm. I, on the other hand, lived in the moment, spontaneous and carefree. He was reserved, I outgoing. As they say, opposites attract.

We were both very conventional, however, similar to many of the students at West Virginia University who wanted to build a better life than their parents had. We had never experimented with drugs, even though we grew up in the "hippie" age. David had his life carefully planned out, and we both wanted to live up to our parents' expectations. I saw my role as primarily being a wife and mother. I planned to teach only until my husband was ready to support a family. We were engaged at Christmas during our senior year of college, and married that summer after graduation (August 3, 1968). We then left for Madison, Wisconsin, where David was enrolled in the doctoral program as a student in organic chemistry, and I was newly employed to teach music at the elementary school in nearby Mazomanie, Wisconsin.

When David completed his doctorate five years later, he accepted a postdoctoral fellowship at the University of

Pennsylvania, and we moved to Philadelphia. At last we felt secure enough economically to begin our family.

Our first daughter was born hydrocephalic. (The old-fashioned term was with "water on the brain".) She was immediately taken to the new Children's Hospital in Philadelphia. Surgery to put in a shunt to relieve the pressure on her brain did not help, and the doctors, after further tests, determined that she had a teratoma. This is a very rare fast-growing brain tumor (one in two million babies are born with this). The tumor was deep in her brain and could not be removed successfully. She lay unconscious in the intensive care unit, hooked up to a respirator and a feeding tube that kept her alive. I stood long hours beside her bed, unable to hold her except for her little feet, since so many tubes were hooked up to her that I could not pick her up or move her. My arms ached so much to hold my baby through all those long silent days. I stood helplessly by her bed, trying to communicate my love for her through the touch of my hands on her small socked feet. I prayed for a miracle.

After Mary Rose had been on the respirator for several weeks, the doctors advised us that there was no hope for her recovery and that we needed to turn off the machines and let her go. We did so with overwhelming grief, but nevertheless certain that it was the right decision. Mary Rose had lived for barely two months. She had only been conscious for one day, on the day that she was born, entering the world with a weak cry. My husband's mother, whose name was also Mary, died just two days after we said good-bye to Mary Rose. The only comfort for me in that time was knowing that my little daughter was now being taken care of by her grandmother up in heaven. My mother-in-law was one of the kindest, most loving people I had ever known. Even in my deep grief, I knew that God had provided this comfort to me and to my mother-in-law by allowing Mary to be with her new little granddaughter in heaven. My mother-in-law lived in West Virginia and had fought a long battle with cancer. Since our baby daughter had never been out of the hospital, and my mother-in-law had been unable to travel, she had never met Mary Rose while she was on earth.

The large medical bills wiped out all of our savings. My husband decided that we could not try to have another child until we had more money saved up. After the terrible sadness of what we had gone through with our first child, I believe he was also afraid to try again, even though genetic counselors told us that there was no reason to fear having another child.

I tried to bury my grief by teaching. While we were still living in Wisconsin, I had gone back to school and earned my master's degree in flute performance. I now taught only flute students in Philadelphia, and I also commuted to Dickinson College in Carlisle, Pennsylvania to teach students there as an adjunct professor. It was a two-hour drive to Carlisle from Philadelphia, so I stayed overnight on the college campus in order to teach two full days a week there. By God's grace and provision, I also had opportunities to play flute in two local orchestras as well, and this kept me busy. Nevertheless, the empty space in my heart left by Mary Rose being gone, and the unfulfilled yearning to hold a baby in my arms, remained a constant source of pain.

Finally, after two years of waiting, David had agreed to try for another child. I was so happy and excited soon after this when I discovered I was pregnant again! But now, facing my present situation, and only eight weeks pregnant, I was terrified. I was alone in the faculty lounge at Settlement Music School in Philadelphia and blood was pouring out of me. Immediately I lay down on the worn brown fabric sofa in this small room, hoping that by putting my feet up I might stop the bleeding. I lay on that couch afraid to move. The room was very small, with no windows. There was only the old brown sofa, a small dark wooden coffee table, and a kitchen sink and coffeemaker against the opposite wall.

When another teacher came in, I asked her to go and tell the secretary in the office downstairs to call my husband to come and take me to the hospital. (This was before we all had cell phones).

I knew it would be at least thirty minutes before my husband could arrive.

I lay there alone in that beige-colored room, desperately hoping the bleeding would stop, all the while weeping and pleading with God. I prayed over and over to the Lord, *"Please, Lord, please let me keep this baby. Please let me keep this baby..."*. Finally, after several minutes of crying out to God, knowing that this was truly out of my control, and that this child was not my possession but His, I finally said, **"Please, Lord, help me accept your will, whatever it is."**

Suddenly the room was filled with this overwhelming Presence of Love and Peace. I was wrapped in a blanket of Love. All my fear was instantly taken away. God's love enveloped me so completely that there was no room left for fear. Then I heard His voice. His voice was the gentlest and most tender voice I have ever heard, and yet at the same time He spoke with such authority that there could be no doubt in my spirit that this was my Lord and Savior speaking.

Jesus said: **"Don't be afraid – everything is in My hands."**

I was filled with His peace and His love. I lay in that little room calmed and quieted. My husband arrived a short time later to take me to the hospital. The bleeding had stopped. I had not lost the baby despite the hemorrhaging. God had answered my prayer.

The doctors told me I must remain on bed rest for at least the next month to prevent more hemorrhaging and a possible miscarriage. I immediately quit all of my teaching and stayed at home for the next several weeks. Most of my time was spent eating crackers for the constant nausea, and reading in bed. David continued to go to work every day at the University of Pennsylvania, but he was just a quick phone call away if I needed him. Thankfully, I had no more heavy bleeding.

At that time I told no one about God speaking to me, not even my husband, but kept it close in my heart. Throughout the rest of my pregnancy God's words to me were an anchor that held me fast.

"*Don't be afraid. Everything is in My hands.*" Drastic changes were soon to come in my life during the next seven months. I would greatly need the anchor of those comforting words from the Lord.

One evening a few weeks after my threatened miscarriage, a friend from out-of-state was visiting us. David had invited a work colleague ("Marsha"), to go out to dinner with us. He told me he wanted to provide our single friend with a date. After dinner we returned home, and I immediately went to bed as I was "spotting" and needed to rest. The three of them went into the living room to watch T.V. and talk.

When I awoke at four a.m. and saw that David had not yet come to bed, I went out to the living room to look for him. I found only our friend sound asleep on the pullout couch. Going back to our bed, I lay awake, wondering where David could be. A short time later my husband arrived home, very surprised to find me wide awake. When I asked him why he was gone so long, he confessed to me that he was carrying on an affair with Marsha, and that he planned to leave me as soon as the baby was born. In fact, he had already told his friend, who had known this woman was not a date for him, but rather someone David wanted him to meet as his (David's) future fiancée.

I was devastated, and in shock at this betrayal by the man I had trusted so completely. I cried all that day, and stayed in bed, not wanting to face anyone. I felt so ashamed. Funny how that can be – David was the one who should have been so ashamed, and I was the one who felt ashamed, afraid that people would find out that my husband planned to leave me for another woman! That same Sunday evening our church had planned a going-away party for us, since my husband had found a new position at Case Western Reserve University in Cleveland, Ohio. We were moving there in a few weeks.

Somehow I got dressed and attended the party. However, I broke down in tears several times when people came up to talk to me, I was in such an emotional state. Everyone thought it was because I was so sad to be leaving them, or related to my pregnant condition. No one suspected the truth--that I had just that morning found out my husband was unfaithful, and planned to leave me. In the beginning I hid this news from my family too. I tried to convince David to stay. David, however, refused to consider ending his affair.

Since I was physically still at risk of a miscarriage and not supposed to do any lifting, friends in Philadelphia helped my husband pack up our belongings, while I stayed with my parents in northwest Pennsylvania. My husband found a house for us to rent in Cleveland from a professor who was on sabbatical--a fully furnished four-bedroom home. I soon joined him in a new city, where I knew no one. I felt more alone than ever, since I could not go out to work yet. My doctors wanted me to stay at home and be careful. Now in the fourth month of my pregnancy, I no longer had morning sickness and was feeling stronger.

I was determined to try and save our marriage. My husband came home in the evening for dinner, but remained emotionally distant. David would go with me to doctor's appointments and to church on Sunday, but otherwise he avoided spending any time with me. He took up running as a sport, a fitting metaphor, since he was also running away from our marriage. My days were spent in near despair. I spent hours driving aimlessly around Cleveland. I cleaned the house diligently, baking my husband's favorite chocolate chip cookies and preparing my best home-cooked meals. I even carefully ironed all of his cotton shirts right out of the dryer (which in the past would stay in the ironing basket for weeks). Alas, nothing changed. David remained indifferent to my efforts.

David did not try to hide his plans to go to a work-related conference in Chicago where he would see Marsha, the woman he now told me he loved instead of me. He had told me that he would stay with me until the baby was born, but his physical presence and economic support did nothing to ease the emotional pain of his betrayal and his continued emotional detachment. One day I opened the credit card bill to discover that he had sent the other woman a dozen roses. I had to sit down quickly, numb with shock, as the reality of my situation sank in. I felt abandoned and alone, but I still could not bring myself to tell my family what was happening. Divorce was unheard of in my family in those days.

Fortunately, I was now well along in the second trimester of my pregnancy and in good health. However, I often woke up in the wee hours of the morning in deep emotional distress. Then I would quietly get out of bed so as not to disturb my sleeping husband, and go into the kitchen to read the Psalms. The Lord comforted me so many times with the beautiful and honest words of David, who had so often also cried out in his heart to the Lord. These wonderful passages of Scripture gave me solace and strength to carry on.

One morning my oldest sister Judy called. She could tell by my voice that something was very wrong. I finally broke down and told her about David's affair and his plans to leave me. She insisted that I come live with her. I was seven months pregnant by this time. She and her husband drove out to Cleveland the very next weekend and brought me back to live with them and their four young children in Zelienople, a town just north of Pittsburgh. Her willingness to do this, even though it meant their small house was now very crowded with three adults and four kids, was a lifeline for me. Her four children were ages eleven, ten, eight and six at the time. I moved into the family den, which had a pullout couch, a room which previously had been her husband's "man-cave".

Later I realized that God had it all planned for us in advance. When I moved in with her, we had no idea that Judy's husband Tom would die six months later, and how much we would need to lean on each other through the next year. For the last two months of my pregnancy I lived with my sister's family and went to her obstetrician, Dr. King.

Sara Elizabeth was born at 6:00 p.m. on Saturday, July 2, 1977, weighing in at six pounds fourteen ounces. She was a beautiful little girl, with dark curly hair, wide-set blue eyes and a high forehead exactly like my husband's. During the delivery, Dr. King even sang the "Hallelujah Chorus" from Handel's *Messiah*! When the doctor laid my sweet daughter on my chest, my eyes filled with tears of happiness as I held her close.

Although she was small for full-term, everything seemed fine for the first twelve hours. But early the next morning my doctor came in and told me they were moving her to Children's Hospital in Pittsburgh for more evaluation, because something was very wrong, and they were not sure exactly what it was. We soon learned that her heart was reversed (dextrocardia), and that she had a very serious heart defect. Her heart had not formed properly while she was in the womb. My new little daughter now lay in an intensive care unit at Children's Hospital with an I.V. giving her nourishment, and hospital nurses caring for her, while I lay in a nearby suburban hospital, unable to hold her and nurse her.

We did not know how long she could survive with this defect, but she was too small and too young to attempt open heart surgery right away. Sara was what they called a "pink" baby, where the blood pumped continually through her heart and back and forth to her lungs, but did not pump out nourishment to the rest of her body very well because of the defects in the heart's inner structure.

Jesus' words of comfort and assurance held me fast – He was my anchor. He had spoken audibly to me and had assured me: *"Everything is in My Hands."*

I could not doubt Him after that powerful experience when I was pregnant, having heard His voice so plainly. Through all those months when my marriage was breaking apart, and now when facing an uncertain future for my daughter, I still knew with absolute certainty: ***Everything is in His hands***. Jesus' words, spoken so clearly to me when I was utterly afraid and alone, comforted me and gave me strength to face the future.

Now I can tell you with confidence, not on my own authority, but relying on God's Word and through His revelation: **you do not need to be afraid** *no matter what your circumstances are*

– **now or ever!** If you have surrendered your life to Him and acknowledge Jesus as your Lord and Savior, He is directing your path. In fact, *He has had you in the palm of His hands since before you were born* (*see* Psalm 139:13). *He is with you, and He will guide you.*

If you have not yet surrendered your life to Him and would like to, you can do it now by saying this prayer: *"Dear Jesus, I ask you to forgive my sins and to accept me into Your kingdom. I acknowledge You as my Lord and Savior, who died for me on the cross. I give you my life now and forevermore. I want to serve You alone, to worship and obey You as my Lord and my God, both now and through all eternity."*

Praise Him for His great mercy and love! You are His child forever!

CHAPTER TWO

GOD'S GRACE IS SUFFICENT

*"And God is faithful, he will not let you be tempted beyond
what you can bear."* (I Cor. 10:13)
*"My grace is sufficient for you, for my power is made perfect
in weakness."* (2 Cor. 12:9)

When my obstetrician, Dr. King, came into my hospital
room the day after my daughter Sara was born and told
me they were sending her to Children's Hospital, not sure exactly
what was wrong but knowing it was very serious, I broke down in
tears. I cried out: "I cannot bear it if she dies too!"

Dr. King replied, "God will not give you more than you can
bear."

I said, "No, that's not true. This would be too much."

But I learned in time that Dr. King was right. God **will** give
us the grace and strength to handle whatever disasters He allows
to happen in our lives. He will sustain you. He tells us: *"Do not
worry about tomorrow,"* and *"each day has enough trouble of its own."*
(Matthew 6::34). It is a reminder to live in the present with Him.
We cannot bear the future – we do not have the strength ahead of
time. He will empower us to bear whatever He puts in our path
at the time we need it. His grace is sufficient.

In the next few days I learned that my daughter Sara had a serious heart defect, and some other issues as well (her heart was reversed and on the right side, and she had polysplenia). The doctors told me that, as a newborn, they did not think she could survive open heart surgery. So after several days of evaluations at Children's Hospital, Sara was sent home with me. It was their hope that she could grow before they tried to operate to repair her heart.

I was delighted to have Sara at home, and to finally be able to hold and nurse my new baby daughter. She was so small that her little tummy could not hold a lot, and I was nursing her every two to three hours in those first few weeks. The joy of having her with me far outweighed any lost sleep. Everyone in the family welcomed this sweet new baby. My sister took care of all the housework, allowing me to devote all of my time to my blue-eyed little package from heaven.

At first Sara gained a little weight, but by two months of age she weighed only eight pounds and had stopped gaining any more. Sara's doctors decided on a desperate measure. They decided to operate to put a small band around her pulmonary artery (the main artery to the lungs), which would then force the blood to go back through her heart and out to the rest of her body to help her grow. It was a primitive remedy and a ticking time bomb, for eventually the band would get too tight as she grew, and would have to be removed. It would buy us some time, however, before the surgeons attempted the full open heart surgery. The doctors explained to me that for Sara, when she was just lying still her heart was working as hard as a normal person's heart would be when they were running at full speed. The doctors also prescribed the medication Lasix to reduce the daily strain on her heart.

At three months of age, Sara had the operation to put the band around her pulmonary artery. I stayed at the hospital in Pittsburgh while Sara was in the intensive care unit. After the operation, her heart was beating very slowly (approximately 35 beats per minute), and the doctors were unsure of her recovery.

Early on the morning after the surgery, my mother was driving down to see Sara and me at Children's Hospital, but first she stopped at my sister's house in Zelienople. She found my sister crying hysterically. Judy's husband, Tom, lay sprawled out in the hallway. He had died of a massive heart attack sometime during the night, while my sister and her children were asleep. They had never heard him fall or even cry out. In the next few days, all of the family gathered to hold a funeral for my brother-in-law and lay him to rest. I also attended at my mother's insistence, even though it tore me up inside to leave my infant daughter alone in the hospital for even a day. Sara remained in intensive care. We did not know if she would survive from even this small operation.

Thankfully, Sara improved, and several days later I was able to bring her home. It was a very different household, however, with my brother-in-law gone. My sister continued her teaching, and the children went off to school as usual, but their father was no longer there, and we were all grieving. God had provided for us, however. Just as my sister had been there for me when I needed a place to run to when I was pregnant, now I could be there for her. I stayed at home in the evenings with the kids while Judy attended night school to get another graduate degree in elementary education, in order to earn more money teaching.

Little Sara, though physically not strong, was a sweet, happy little baby. She brought smiles to all of us. My oldest nephew Tommy, who was only eleven when his father died, especially spent a lot of time playing with Sara and taking care of her. Sara loved his constant attention. She was generally a sunny-natured baby, her blue eyes bright and engaged. I could not bear to see her cry for too long or too hard. I was so afraid that her overtaxed heart would literally give out, and so I confess I spoiled her. Sara grew very slowly but steadily. We had regular monthly trips to the Children's Hospital at Pittsburgh for her check-ups.

Despite the grief over the loss of my brother-in-law and the anxiety over my daughter's health, my sister and I were able to share many happy times with the kids, from walks in the snow to visits to the kids' favorite candy store. I don't know how I would have managed without my sister's help. Judy and I were able to provide emotional support for each other during a period of great stress and upheaval. There were many tears, but fun-filled days too. We were held securely in God's loving arms.

"My grace is sufficient for you, for my power is made perfect in weakness." (2 Cor. 12:9)

CHAPTER THREE

ALL OF OUR DAYS ARE NUMBERED BEFORE ONE OF THEM CAME TO BE

"All your days are numbered before one of them came to be."
(Psalm 139:16)

*T*he day arrived when we could wait no longer for Sara's open-heart surgery. Sara was twenty-one months old. We were now living with my Mom and Dad, after a year in Zelienople with my sister. Judy had decided to move closer to the rest of our family after the death of her husband. She had bought a new home near Knox, in northwest Pennsylvania where we all grew up. Now both of my sisters lived within ten miles of my parents, and also my two brothers and their families were only a few more miles away. It allowed us all to see more of each other and have the support of a close family.

We could not put off Sara's surgery any longer. The band on her pulmonary artery had been in place for eighteen months and had outworn its usefulness in helping her to grow; it now constricted the blood flow to her lungs. She could not walk (that would take more strength than she had), but she did manage to scoot around on her little behind using her arms and legs to help propel her forward. Sara was always determined to try and do everything she saw everyone else doing. One day she managed to pull herself up and climb into my Dad's large upholstered recliner. She sat there so proud of herself for accomplishing a task I would have thought impossible for her--and if I had seen her as she was doing it, I would have stopped her from trying! She could play contentedly for hours, sitting quietly with her dolls and toys. "Hot, hot", she would exclaim, as she took her doll-size saucepan and poured some imaginary food onto her doll's plate, imitating my warnings. When I played my flute, she would blow into her little plastic recorder. Opening a book, she would carefully scribble small lines and circles in it.

Of course I had known this day would come, even though I would not allow myself to think about it ahead of time. Sara had gone through a heart catheterization procedure just two months before this in order for the doctors to view her heart closely. We knew that they had to try to repair the heart, which was so overworked, and would soon fail otherwise. The doctors told me that her chances of surviving the operation were 50/50 at best. I had the feeling that even then they were trying to soften the blow, and that they considered her chances even less. Nevertheless, a mother always hopes – who can imagine the alternative?

We checked Sara into Children's Hospital of Pittsburgh on a sunny Saturday afternoon in April. The open heart surgery was scheduled for early Monday morning, but there were tests and evaluations to be done before the actual surgery took place. I was allowed to stay in the hospital room with her. My brother-in-law Gus brought us some French fries from McDonald's, which Sara loved. Not being able to say the "fr" yet, she called them "en ies". The hospital had toys and playrooms, and we passed the time, with family visiting, until Sunday night. That evening, I was not allowed to give her anything to eat or drink, as her stomach had to be empty when she went into surgery early the next morning. Since I was still nursing her at night before she went to sleep, she could not understand why Mom put her down in the hospital crib without that nourishing comfort and food. Finally she fell asleep, but it was a long anxious night for me. Early the next morning around six-thirty a.m., the nurses came and took her away. I could only kiss her on the forehead before giving her up to them.

My mother, my younger brother and his wife, and even my husband (from whom I had been separated since before Sara was born), arrived at the hospital to wait with me on the day of the operation. We waited through the long, long day while she was in surgery. I prayed and hoped, sitting and then pacing, unable to focus on anything, and then I prayed and hoped some more. Finally, about four in the afternoon, the social worker came to meet with us, and said: "Sara is not doing well". Then the surgeon came in about a half-hour later and told us her little heart was just not strong enough, and had given out soon after the surgery was completed. They asked me if I wanted to go see her.

I went into the cold, still hospital room where her body lay covered with a white sheet, with only her pale little face showing. I kissed her on the forehead to say good-bye. I was unable to think or feel, moving as a robot, in a state of profound shock and entirely numb. I could not believe she was truly gone. My mother, brother and sister-in-law must have helped me out of the hospital. I remember nothing of the journey home. We were all overcome with grief, and silence was surely the only conceivable response to such desolation.

The next day we prepared for her funeral, to be held at the same little church where I had grown up. This was a dear little white clapboard church in the country. The small rectangular sanctuary had three plain stained-glass windows on either side, and several rows of well-polished wooden pews. The minister stood on a raised platform in the front, and a picture of Jesus hung on the solid white wall directly behind him. An upright piano was to the minister's right, along with several chairs for the choir. The church was surrounded by pleasant green fields, with a small cemetery directly behind it where my first daughter's gravestone already lay, marked and put in place almost five years before.

I turned to Scriptures in my pain. God took me directly to Psalm 139, the very Psalm I had used for Sara's birth announcement. At her birth, I had used verses 13 and 14 which say: *"For you created my inmost being; you knit me together in my mother's womb. I praise you because I am fearfully and wonderfully made".* Now the Lord led me to these words in verse 16: *"Your eyes saw my unformed body; all the days ordained for me were written in your book before one of them came to be."* I knew with certainty that Jesus was telling me the amount of time Sara had lived on earth was exactly within God's plan.

These words comforted me despite my pain. I already knew I would see her again in heaven--I had been assured of that in faith from years before when my first daughter died. Now, in the depths of my grief, I understood that I could still trust God IN ALL. He had given me a great gift in allowing me to mother Sara for nearly two years, when I could so easily have lost her in that threatened miscarriage when I was eight weeks pregnant. Truly everything **is** in His hands.

All of her days were numbered before one of them came to be. This meant also that the length of her life was known and in God's plan before she was even born. I knew that this was also according to His <u>good</u> plan, because, knowing God, I knew His perfect goodness, and that He is all loving. Even in my grief, I knew I could trust Him totally. It did not take away my sorrow, but God's promise to me in these verses from the 139th Psalm did give me solid assurance and comfort. I was standing on a Rock, a Rock that could not be moved. He would hold me fast always. Just as Jesus' earlier words to me that *"everything is in My Hands"* had been my strong anchor, these words showing His plan for Sara's life and mine steadied and strengthened me.

At her funeral, I told everyone with certainty: "We are just saying good-bye to her for a little while. We will see her again in heaven." My last strong happy image of my daughter Sara remains fixed in my mind's eye, from the night before her surgery. My petite little girl, dressed in a pink cotton top and matching pants, is standing up in the hospital stroller and holding on tightly to the front handlebar, her blue eyes sparkling with joy as we race down an empty hospital corridor. I am behind her pushing as fast as I can in such a setting (and much faster than permitted if hospital personnel had seen us). Her laughter rings out as she "runs" through the air. *Now she can run freely in heaven.*

Although I would weep for many hours in the days and months ahead, these words were not empty promises but convictions in my spirit, planted there by His Holy Spirit. *I would see her again in Heaven.* **These were things I was sure of by His grace.**

Believe His Word, dear ones–Jesus will never fail you!! He will never leave you nor forsake you once you have given your life to Him. He knows your beginning and your end. He has chosen you already to be with Him. As it says in Romans 8:29: *"For those whom God foreknew he also predestined to be conformed to the likeness of His Son, that He might be the firstborn among many brothers and sisters".*

What amazing love! *"Amazing love, and can it be - that Thou my Lord has died for me."* (Hymn by Charles Wesley, Amazing Love).

CHAPTER FOUR

STARTING ANEW: GOD WILL PROVIDE

"Therefore I tell you, do not worry about your life, what you will eat or drink; or about your body, what you will wear... for your heavenly Father knows that you need them." (Matt. 6:25-32)

A few months after my daughter Sara's passing, I moved to New York City. I needed to move away from my family in Pennsylvania and find a place to begin a new career. There were too many memories of Sara to continue living at home with my parents, and also not enough things to keep me busy as a classical musician in this rural area. I wanted to play the flute and to be in a place where classical music thrived. Naively, I thought New York City would be similar to living in Philadelphia, where I had lived for three years, only just a little bigger city in size. Was I in for a surprise!!

A married couple with whom I had been good friends in Philadelphia now lived in the northern tip of Manhattan (in the Inwood neighborhood). They invited me to stay with them until I could find a job and a place to live. Finding a job was the easy part. Within two weeks I started working as a secretary for

Columbia Artists Management, down on 57th Street right across from Carnegie Hall in the center of Manhattan. It was the perfect place for me during that first year in the city. I got to hear many of the finest musicians in the world for free, courtesy of CAMI (Columbia Artists Management). My boss, Larry Tucker, was the assistant to the president of the company, and worked with such famous artists as Mstislav Rostropovitch, Marilyn Horne, Shirley Verrett, Martha Argerich, Andre Previn, and others. I helped to arrange their travel itineraries and had the opportunity to meet some of the greatest classical musicians in the world. Even with those artists that Columbia didn't manage, I could easily walk across the street to Carnegie Hall and listen to inspiring performances by singers such as Dietrich Fischer-Dieskau and Luciano Pavarotti.

It was a time of learning and excitement for me in a city like no other, a city of unlimited energy and ambition. At the corner restaurant near my apartment, the waiter would have ready my breakfast of eggs, whole wheat toast, and home fries two minutes after I sat down at the counter. Everyone and everything moved faster in New York! There was always so much to see and do! It was stimulating and invigorating, a constant energy "high".

At first, though, I often found myself lonely. I wanted a husband, and longed to have more children to help fill those large holes in my heart left by the loss of my daughters Mary Rose and Sara Elizabeth. A wise priest once told me that losing a child is like an "inner amputation"--similar to losing an arm or leg, but no one can see it from the outside. That described perfectly how I felt. Losing anyone you dearly love leaves an empty place inside, but there is something so much more painful when you see your child die and the "natural order" of life is disrupted, even turned on its head. You go on, but your vision of the future and seeing your generations to come, is cut off. Every time I saw small children it reminded me of my loss, but most especially I found it hard to bear when I would see a little girl of age three or four. Even passing by the little girls dresses in a department store would remind me of my daughter's next stage that I was now missing (Sara had died at age two).

For the first time in my life I was living alone. I had rented a small apartment in New York City at the northernmost tip of Manhattan. I wondered if I would ever be able to trust a man again after the betrayal by my first husband. I desperately wanted to have more children, but I was afraid to give my heart to anyone or commit to marrying again. This fear also led me to compromise with myself on what had previously been a moral certitude, since I had waited until my marriage for sexual intimacy, only to find myself betrayed and then abandoned. I could not imagine the pain if I married and that happened to me again.

One day I was feeling very sorry for myself and feeling very lonely, and I said to God, *"Who loves me?"*

Jesus answered me immediately in my spirit. He said, *"Who do you love?"*

Instantly I was turned around in my spirit. Who did I love? As I thought about my family and friends and all the people I knew and loved, I was strengthened and lifted up. No longer was I self-pitying. I was encouraged and now wanted to show love to someone else, rather than waiting for an imaginary "Prince Charming" to come and rescue me.

God was showing me how to be happy, how to live. He was saying: *"Take your eyes off of yourself, Kathy. Focus on others' needs and how you can love them. This is the way to live."* As Scripture reads: *"Be devoted to one another in love. Honor one another above yourselves."* (Romans 12:10).

When I turned to God in my sorrow and grief, He also showed me that I needed to be thankful for what I had, rather than falling into that pit of depression by looking at what I didn't have. Although I would always feel my loss, I learned to be thankful for the time that I had had with Sara, and thankful for my many memories of mothering her and getting to know her, rather than staying in that pit of despair and mourning for what was not.

It was God's gift to me that Sara was with me here on earth for almost two years. I had nearly lost her at eight weeks when I hemorrhaged, and if I had miscarried then, I would never have known the joy of mothering her at all. I learned to start thanking God for all He has given me and to rejoice in His gifts, both past and present, instead of remaining stuck in the mire of feeling sorry for myself.

"In everything give thanks, for this is the will of God concerning you." (I Thessalonians 5:18).

CHAPTER FIVE

GOD'S PERFECT TIMING

"Therefore I tell you, do not worry about your life, what you will eat or drink; or about your body, what you will wear... your heavenly Father knows that you need them." (Matthew 6:25,32)

Living in Manhattan and working as a secretary and freelance musician, I sometimes found myself pretty short on cash. My apartment was on 207th Street near Broadway, the last subway stop on the "A" train. One evening I jumped on the subway to go downtown to meet a friend for dinner. I looked in my purse, and to my dismay found I had absolutely no money! I did not want to ask my friend to pay for dinner. We were meeting at *The Magic Pan*, a restaurant in midtown where you could still get a meal for less than ten dollars at that time (the early 80's). I asked Jesus what to do. Then I opened my small pocket New Testament for some words of comfort. A ten-dollar bill fell out! I laughed – all was well! I had enough money to pay for my meal and enjoy some time with my friend.

A few months later, I was at home in my apartment on a blustery snowy Saturday morning a week after Christmas, and feeling pretty despondent. In a couple of hours I needed to catch the Hudson River Metro train to Brewster, New York, in order to take a music lesson with Julius Baker, the first flutist with the New York Philharmonic. But I had no money for the train fare, nor any other way to get there.

I was still in my bathrobe when the doorbell rang. There stood Charles, the tall, gangly, very shy organist from the Presbyterian Church in my neighborhood. His thinning sandy hair was blown by the wind, his eyeglasses were wet with snowflakes, his ears were red with the cold, and his heavy jacket was zipped up tightly with the collar turned up against the wind. I had played flute for his church's Christmas Eve service the week before. He handed me a personal check for twenty-five dollars. He apologized for coming by so early in the morning, but told me he had felt compelled to come by and make sure I got this check right away. He had come out in the middle of a snowstorm just to give me this money! My eyes widened with surprise. His check was the exact amount I needed to cover the round trip train fare to take me up to Brewster later that morning for my flute lesson. I thanked him profusely. What a gift! Praise God for that dear man's obedience to the Holy Spirit's urging! God's timing was perfect – as always!

There are so many instances where I have seen God's provision, both in the smallest things and in the largest things. When He says He has every hair on our head numbered (Matthew 10:30), do not doubt it, dear friends! He truly cares about even the tiniest details in our lives, because He truly cares about us! His love is a deeper and more complete love than we can experience in any human relationship, for He knows us fully. Every thought is known, every *"word on our tongue before we speak it"* (Psalm 139:4).

Another example of God's amazing provision and care had happened to me some years before, right after I graduated from college. I was newly married and living in Madison, Wisconsin. My husband was beginning graduate school at the University. I was starting my first job teaching public school music in a small town nearby (Mazomanie, WI). We had just moved into graduate student housing off campus, and had barely met our new neighbors who lived across the hall.

All through college I had played the flute, and I missed playing in a group. When I saw a notice of an opening in the Madison Symphony Orchestra to play third flute and piccolo, I rushed to sign up for the audition. I practiced hard and prepared a solo piece on the flute, but since I did not own a piccolo, I could not prepare anything on that instrument.

A week later I walked into the audition. Sitting in the room were only two people. An older man with silver hair and a neatly-trimmed salt-and-pepper beard stood up and introduced himself as the principal flutist with the orchestra, Mr. Robert Cole. Mr. Cole taught flute at the University of Wisconsin and had formerly played with the Philadelphia Orchestra. Beside him sat a pretty, dark-haired woman in her mid-thirties, who played second flute. They would be the judges to evaluate me.

First I played my prepared piece on the flute. After hearing my flute solo, Mr. Cole asked me to sight-read an orchestral excerpt on the piccolo. I told him I did not have a piccolo. He raised his eyebrows in surprise, but being a gentleman, he offered me his piccolo to play while he picked up his flute to play alongside of me.

I had not played a piccolo since my high school marching band days, nor had I ever seen the orchestral piece Mr. Cole put on the music stand in front of me. But, undaunted, I put Mr. Cole's piccolo to my mouth and played the technically difficult music without a single mistake! Every note was in tune and in exact time with Mr. Cole, who was playing the part along with me on his flute. I won the audition! I was thrilled!

Now I look back in wonder at my chutzpah in taking the audition, when I didn't even own a piccolo and hadn't played one in over four years! However, God was with me, giving me the courage and confidence to do what most people would consider foolhardy in taking an audition without even owning the right instrument! At the time I did not yet know Jesus personally, nor even remember to ask God for any help, but He was still directing my path. It was His purpose guiding me before I even knew to ask.

After winning the audition, I next needed a piccolo, and quickly! I went home to our apartment. As I was unlocking my door, my neighbor across the hall came out of his apartment. I told him about winning the position in the orchestra and mentioned that I now needed a piccolo.

His eyes lit up as he said, "My grandfather who lives in Florida wants to sell his Haynes silver piccolo, since he no longer plays it. I will ask him to send it to you if you are interested."

I could not believe my good fortune! Just like that, I had my piccolo! (It turned out to be the perfect instrument for me, too- -God's perfect provision.)

The piccolo arrived a few days later, in time for my first rehearsal. For the next several years I played that Haynes piccolo in the Madison Symphony Orchestra. As I sat in the woodwind section that first season, playing beside members of the faculty from the University of Wisconsin, I gained the confidence I needed to go on to study with Mr. Cole and earn a master's degree in flute performance. (This was God's hand guiding me even then, before I knew Him.)

How the Lord blessed me, providing for me and granting me my heart's desire! First, I was able to play beside and learn from professional musicians of national reputation in the orchestra. This then led me to study with Mr. Cole (who himself had studied and played with William Kincaid, recognized as the greatest American flute teacher in the 20th century). And all of this happened because I walked "blindly" into that audition (or more truly, God had directed my steps).

I am in awe of how God works. He both prepares and plans for us *"all good works that we are to walk in"*.* His love is complete and perfect! We can trust Him to know what we need and to provide for us *always* and in *all ways.* Don't be afraid to follow Him, wherever He leads!

* *"For we are God's handiwork, created in Christ Jesus to do good works, which God prepared in advance for us to do." (*Ephesians 2:10)

CHAPTER SIX

NEW EVERY MORNING: GOD FORGIVES ALL PAST SINS AND GIVES US A NEW BEGINNING

*"As far as the east is from the west,
so far has he removed our transgressions from us."*
(Psalm 103:12)

I have learned that God's forgiveness is total and his love is unconditional. He will not hold anything against us; He gladly forgives us of our sins, even before we come to Him to ask His forgiveness. After all, He is outside of time--He created time! Therefore He has foreknowledge of all events, and sees *"all of our days before one of them came to be."* (Psalm 139:16)

There was a time when I was afraid to even ask God to forgive me. I felt so guilty, so ashamed of what I had done, that I did not feel worthy to approach Him. I couldn't forgive myself. Knowing what I knew of God and His love for me, I still had chosen to disobey Him. I was in a miserable state.

After my divorce from David, I was living alone in New York City. As I described in earlier chapters, my ex-husband and I had had two daughters, both of whom had died of birth defects at very young ages. I desperately wanted to be a mother again and to carry a healthy child. Yet I was also deeply afraid to marry again -- afraid to trust a man after my ex-husband's adulterous affair and his decision to continue with the other woman even while I was pregnant with our second child.

So it happened that I found myself "accidentally" getting pregnant with no intention or desire to marry the father. I could blame no one but myself. I could not bring myself to even ask God's forgiveness for getting into this mess, since I had purposely chosen to disobey Him. I could not even read my Bible.

Now newly pregnant, I was too ashamed to tell anyone. On this bright summer day, I was travelling to Long Island to attend a noontime ceremony at an Episcopal monastery where my cousin was being installed as a monk. During the service, the entire Psalm 121 was read aloud, and the words bore deep into my soul. God had often used those words to comfort me in the past:

"The Lord is thy keeper... the sun will not smite you by day, nor the moon by night... [I] will watch, over thy going out and thy coming in from this time forth, and even for evermore (Psalm 121: 5-8, King James Version).

My heart was torn with grief, since I felt I could not turn to God for help; I was too full of guilt for my conscious rebellion. I went home with the words of Psalm 121 reverberating loudly in my head.

I drove back to the city and was back in my apartment later that afternoon. The doorbell rang. My good friend Pat, who is a Jewish Christian, had come by for a visit. When I opened the door, she handed me a small book. It was the Union Prayer Book, a book of prayers and scriptures used for worship in the synagogue. She said that God had told her to give me this book. I was stunned. Pat had often given me devotional books before, but never with that instruction. She had no idea of how I was struggling that day nor my state of mind, since I had not told her that I was pregnant.

Taking the book from her hand, the pages fell open to the words of Psalm 121. Pat said in surprise, "I had bookmarked another page for you that I thought you would like, but the Lord must have meant for you to read this one!"

I could barely hold back the tears. I knew instantly that God was calling out to me, wooing me back to Him with these assurances that He loved me and that He was watching over me. He was telling me very clearly that whatever I had done, *it could not separate me from Him.*

My pride kept me from confessing to my friend my predicament right then. I was afraid of her condemnation as well, so I simply thanked her profusely. I did admit to her, however, that I had been feeling estranged from God, and that her message from Him showed me that He did not want me to stay away!

Later that evening when I was alone, I confessed it all to Him, and weeping, received Him again into my heart. A few weeks later I miscarried, but God's peace was with me in spite of the pain of that event.

Is there anything holding you back right now from receiving His wholehearted love and forgiveness? If there is, please know this: there is NOTHING you can do that God will not forgive! His love for you is complete and unconditional. He is simply waiting for you to come to Him. *"With arms wide open, He welcomes you! It is no secret, what God can do."* ("It Is No Secret" by C.S. Hamblen).

Just in case you are still saying to yourself, *"Well, God may be able to forgive you of your sin, but I have done something so unforgivable and horrible that God cannot possibly forgive me."* Dear friend, He has already forgiven you, and is ready to welcome you into His arms!

I once read the story of a man who was going to be executed for the horrific crime of sexually abusing and killing a young boy. He had refused all appeals, saying that if he ever got out of jail, he knew he would not be able to stop himself from doing more unspeakable crimes, and so he wanted to die. However, in his last words before being executed, he said this: "I thought there was no hope, no peace for me. <u>I was wrong</u>. There is hope and peace in Jesus Christ."

Dear friend, this man was forgiven and restored to a right mind by Jesus Christ. Before he died, he found Jesus' love for him and accepted Him as his Savior.

Is this not proof enough for you that God will forgive you too, no matter what you have done? Be assured, He has already seen the worst in you, and He has paid the price for you by His death on the cross in your place. **You are worth all to Him.**

"Softly and tenderly Jesus is calling, calling for you and for me. Softly and tenderly Jesus is calling, calling "oh sinner, come home. Come home, come home – ye who are weary, come home." ("Softly and Tenderly" by Will L. Thompson).

Go to Jesus – He will take all your burdens and bear them for you. **He is the only one who can.** He is the Savior of the world, the Lord and King of the universe. All praise to Him forever!!

"Cast all your anxiety on Him because He cares for you." (I Peter 5:7)

CHAPTER SEVEN

JESUS IS
ALWAYS WITH THE BELIEVER

"And surely I am with you always, to the very end of the age"
(Matthew 28:20)

*I*t was a brilliantly sunny Saturday in July. I was driving across
Pennsylvania on Interstate 80, hurrying to get to my parents'
home. Today was my younger brother's birthday, and his wife
was holding an afternoon barbecue and family party. I had left
New York City in a rental car very early that morning. Usually
I rented the lowest-priced subcompacts, but this time the rental
company had given me an upgrade to a bigger car because they
didn't have any of the smaller cars left on the lot. I had not gotten
enough sleep and was fairly tired, so I stopped early on for coffee
at a McDonalds at an Interstate 80 exit in New Jersey. However,
their coffee wasn't brewed yet, and the server only had a pot of
last night's coffee to offer. I took it, but when I got back on the
road I discovered that the cardboard cup of coffee was too bitter
for me to drink.

After driving for nearly four hours, I was midway across
Pennsylvania and had not yet eaten anything. I stopped for gas
and picked up a candy bar and a Snapple sweet iced tea. After

getting back in the car, I uncharacteristically snapped on my seatbelt even though I rarely used a seatbelt. I had not been wearing one through the earlier part of my drive. The sweet tea did not have the effect that a strong coffee would have, and the candy bar didn't help. I found myself getting very sleepy, and I momentarily nodded off a couple of times as I continued across the hills of central Pennsylvania in the late morning sun. However, there were no more places to stop for coffee in this isolated section of the interstate, so I kept driving.

I moved into the left lane to pass a truck. I was going about 75 miles per hour. Suddenly I woke up realizing my car was veering right into the side of the semi truck travelling alongside of me in the right lane. There was no time to think – I turned the steering wheel hard to the left as I slammed into the truck in its middle section. My car tumbled over the guardrail and down the side of a sloping grassy hill. As the car rolled over and over, I felt the force of my head hitting the ceiling very hard several times, and I briefly wondered why the airbag had not deployed. But the seatbelt still held me in my seat. The car finally came to a stop upside down at the bottom of this long grassy gentle incline. Apparently the airbag had not been activated since I had hit the semi on the right passenger side of my car and not from the front. When the car stopped, I was hanging upside down but still strapped in by my seatbelt. I turned off the engine, unhooked my seatbelt, opened the car door and crawled out onto the green grass. As I tried to get my bearings, I noticed multiple small scratches on my legs below my shorts from a broken compact mirror that had flown out of my purse on the seat beside me. I was not yet aware of my other injuries.

A young man ran down the hill calling out: "Are you all right? Don't move, don't move!" When he came up to me he said, "I can't believe you are alive! I was right behind you and saw you hit the truck. Don't move! I just took a course on accidents in college. Don't move!"

A minute later, two women who also had seen the accident stopped their car and came down the hill. They told me they were both nurses. I said I did not seem hurt, but they said that there was blood running down the back of my head (it must have been from hitting inside the roof of the car as it rolled over several times going down the hill). They asked me what year it was and who was President. Satisfied with my answers, they went back to their car and brought out a shiny silver space blanket which would reflect the sun and protect me from the hot noontime rays.

The three of them (the two nurses and the college boy) held the silver blanket over me while we waited for the ambulance. The truck driver had also pulled over and walked down the hill to see what had happened. He said that when he felt the thump of my car hitting the truck, at first he thought he had blown a tire. I asked him if his truck was damaged and he kind of laughed and said it was not. (I guess it was funny that I would ask about his truck as I sat there with blood running down through my hair and onto the back of my neck.)

It was amazing to me how just the right people stopped to help me, as well as the more amazing fact that I had hit a truck and gone over the guardrail right where there was a long gentle grassy incline, instead of any of the many places where there were rocky cliffs or large trees, or similarly more dangerous places along the highway. The car was totaled, but I ended up with only a concussion requiring several stitches, a bruised left shoulder where the seatbelt had held me in, and a few scratches on my legs from the broken compact mirror.

How easily it could have been the end of my earthly life that day! What if I had not buckled my seatbelt a short time before? What if I had been driving the cheap compact car that I usually rented instead of a larger car with a roof strong enough to not cave in when rolling over and over? What if I had rolled the car into another car? God had kept me alive--His purposes for me here on earth were not done yet! Hallelujah, praise the Lord! Thank you, Jesus, for your loving protection and care!

"All your days are numbered, before one of them came to be." (Psalm 139).

"The Lord is my rock and my fortress and my deliverer" (2 Samuel 22:2).

CHAPTER EIGHT

WE CAN DEPEND ON GOD'S PROTECTION IN ANY SITUATION

"For he will command his angels concerning you to guard you in all your ways." (Psalm 91:11)

God has protected me in so many frightening situations. I cannot count them all, but I expect in heaven I will look back over my life and I will be surprised at how many times God has kept me safe when I did not even know I was in danger! So often I have seen His loving hand guarding me. One very clear instance is the following story.

In the spring of 1993 I decided to visit Israel. For several years I had wanted to make a pilgrimage to Israel to visit the places so dear to Jesus and central in His earthly life. I wanted to go alone so that I could follow God's leading and not be hurried through by a tour group or guide. Since I needed to save money, I planned to stay in hostels while I was there. My main goal was to see Jerusalem, so I arranged to stay at a French nunnery right outside of the Damascus Gate in the Old City of Jerusalem for the first few days. Then I planned to move to a nearby Anglican hostel for a total of ten days altogether in the city.

After a nonstop eleven-hour flight from New York's JFK Airport on El Al Airlines, I arrived in Tel Aviv at around 5 a.m. Israeli time. I then took a forty-five minute taxi ride to Jerusalem. Arriving at the convent, the lone nun on duty showed me to my small single-bed room, sparsely furnished. I was only a few steps from the entrance to the walled Old City at the Damascus Gate. Dropping my unopened bag on the floor and grabbing only my backpack, I immediately ran out the front door of the nunnery and went through the Damascus Gate into the Old City to begin exploring.

It was still very early, not yet 6 a.m. Finding some broad stone steps which led up to the top of the forty-foot high stone wall that encircled the Old City, I excitedly began walking along on the top of the wall (which was at least three feet across). I was entranced with the magnificent view of the whole city in the light of the rising sun. Without a map, however, I was soon lost. I came to a place where the wall was cracked apart and broken down. I could go no further on top of the wall, and so I walked down several worn stone steps into a section of the city that I later learned was called the Muslim Quarter.

I was an American woman alone in a part of the city that was not friendly to young single American women, but I was ignorant of that fact. It was too early for people to be out walking about and the streets were deserted. I strolled slowly past very modest homes packed tightly together. There was a single clothesline behind one house with a few articles of clothing hanging out to dry. I walked on, marveling at how the early morning sun cast such a beautiful golden light on everything around me in this hallowed city.

Suddenly I heard a boy's voice calling out, "What are you doing here?"

I looked up to see a young Arab boy, around age 12 or 13, watching me from a second-story window. He then came down out of his house and ran up alongside of me. A wiry, dark-skinned boy about my height (5'4"), he was dressed in a faded dark T-shirt and tan knee-length shorts. His eyes fastened on me with belligerence. No one else was around. I told him that I had just arrived in the city and was out exploring. I had read about the need to dress modestly in the Old City, and so I was wearing a blue-flowered culotte skirt that covered my knees, and a long-sleeved white blouse.

With a sly smirk he grabbed the edge of my culottes and said, "Pretty skirt".

This made me uncomfortable, but I just silently shook my head "no" and pulled away from him, walking faster to put him behind me.

As I hurried on, I suddenly felt something slam against my back. But it was the strangest thing. I felt his body hit against me, but all the force was taken out of it. My body was unaffected, completely unmoved; I was not knocked over, nor even a bit shaken. The boy had apparently stepped back and taken a running leap to try to knock me to the ground, probably intending to steal my backpack. However, instead, he was the one who had fallen backwards to the ground.

I turned around and yelled in a loud voice: "Get away from me! Get away from me!"

I hoped that others would hear me and come out to help, but no one did. My attacker was flat on his back on the ground. I walked quickly on. My last memory of the boy was seeing the very stunned and confused expression on his face as he looked up at me. He did not try to get up to follow me.

Afterwards I realized I had foolishly walked into a dangerous place. I am convinced that God sent a guardian angel to protect me there, and that is why the boy's attack had no effect on me. For although I had felt his body hit my back, I had also felt completely unmoved and as strong as a firmly rooted tree trunk. God had protected me.

I walked more carefully in the city from then on, not venturing again into the Muslim Quarter alone. Later, other experiences in and around the city of Jerusalem helped me understand that in the Muslim culture, a single American woman travelling alone was often viewed as a prostitute. Probably that boy was "testing" me, since it must have been strange to him to see an American woman alone in his area of the city. But I escaped unharmed, due to God's protection.

"If I make my bed in the depths, you are there. If I rise on the wings of the dawn, if I settle on the far side of the sea, even there your hand will guide me, your right hand will hold me fast." (Psalm 139:8-10.)

CHAPTER NINE

THE LITTLE RED CAR: GOD DESIGNS THINGS, GIVES US SURPRISE GIFTS IN HIS LOVE FOR US

"Every good and perfect gift is from above, coming down from the Father of the heavenly lights, who does not change like shifting shadows." (James 1:17)

*M*y father was ill. I needed a car to be able to make the six-hour trip from New York City to northwest Pennsylvania to see him more often. Living in New York City, it was easy to get around without a car and I had not owned one for some time. As I drove home only for the holidays, renting a car sufficed on those few occasions when I needed one. But now it was different with my Dad seriously ill. I wanted to go home more frequently. So I prayed. I needed a car, but I had only $800 saved. Little cars appealed to me, and my favorite color for a car was red. But I did not ask God for those particulars. I asked Him for a car with only two conditions: (1) that it would get me safely to and from northwest Pennsylvania, and (2) that it would cost no more than $800.

A few days later I was walking out of the small Episcopal church in northern Manhattan where I had been practicing the organ to prepare for next Sunday's service, and as I came down the steps to the street I noticed a little red car parked on the street directly in front of the church. There was a large handwritten "for sale" sign in the side window. Copying down the phone number, I hurried back to my apartment to call, praying that if this was the car for me, its price would be $800. When a woman answered, I first asked how much she wanted for the car. She said, "Eight hundred dollars." I was ecstatic! I knew this was the answer to my prayer! We agreed to meet when she got off work.

Later that afternoon, I walked back to the church to meet her. Standing by the car was a pretty young Latino woman in her 20's, with shoulder-length dark hair, fashionably dressed in a dark gray business suit and wearing black heels. She greeted me with a warm smile, and we introduced ourselves. The car was a French make, a little Renault Le Car with a manual transmission. That suited me perfectly. I loved the feel of a stick shift and the sense of independence it gave me compared to an automatic transmission. Also my mother had first taught me how to drive on her old Ford with a stick shift on the steering wheel, and remembering learning to drive that old car brought back many happy memories. I have never liked automatic transmissions, but in Manhattan the cars I rented always had automatic transmissions! I looked longingly through the window of the little red car, noticing the stick shift on the floor. I couldn't wait to try it out!

The young woman handed me the keys and I got into the driver's seat while she took the passenger side. I started up the engine and then reached for the smooth knob of the stick shift with my right hand. After working through the gears, I pulled out of the parking space into the heavy street traffic in upper Manhattan. The young woman sat beside me in the passenger seat as I drove slowly around the block. I then pulled into the same parking space that we had left less than ten minutes before.

I turned to her and said, "I'll take it!"

The woman, surprised, asked, "Don't you want to take the car on the Henry Hudson Parkway or out on the highway to see how it runs there?" (I had told her I needed the car to drive to Pennsylvania.)

I said, "Oh no, it's fine. I know it will be perfect for me since I asked God, and this is the car He has chosen for me. I am sure it will be just fine."

We completed the paperwork, and I was the proud owner of one of the cutest little red cars I had ever seen. The fact that it was used, with the red paint faded in spots, and other signs of wear in the upholstery didn't bother me. In my eyes it was adorable!

I drove the car home to Pennsylvania the following week. My Dad (who loved engines of any kind), looked the car over and said, "Why, it only has a sewing machine size engine in it!"

Laughing, I nodded my head. It was true – the car's top speed was eighty miles an hour, which I had quickly discovered on my drive across Interstate 80. However, even in that I saw God's provision. Speed delights me. I will drive as fast as I can get away with. If that car had been capable of higher speeds I surely would have gotten several speeding tickets, or even possibly had an accident.

The little red car held up for the next several years as I drove back and forth from New York to Pennsylvania to see my Dad. God had not only provided me with the car I needed, He had also given me a car that suited my personality exactly. I smiled every time I looked at it – it was the perfect surprise gift.*

---

*Addendum: Some years later (when the little red Renault was no longer), I needed another car. I was living in a large apartment complex at the time in Fairfax, Virginia. I prayed about a car, again knowing I had a tight budget. I walked out of my door one morning and there in the parking lot was a little red car for sale (this time a domestic brand, not a Renault), and once again I found God's provision perfect. (Why are we surprised?)

I drove that car for the next two years. He will provide for you! It may not be in a car appearing in your driveway – God fits His surprises uniquely to each person, as He knows us so very well. But I guarantee you that He will provide if you will trust Him. As James says: "*But he must ask in faith without any doubting, for the one who doubts is like the surf of the sea, driven and tossed by the wind.*" (James 1:6)

CHAPTER TEN

THE HOLY SPIRIT GUIDES ME AND RESIDES WITHIN ME

"When the Advocate comes, whom I will send to you from the Father—the Spirit of truth who goes out from the Father— he will testify about me. (John 15:26)

The Holy Spirit lives within me. This is Jesus' promise to those of us who believe and accept Him as our Savior and Lord. We are in fact "sealed by the Holy Spirit to be His forever" (*See* 2 Cor. 5:5: *"Now the one who has fashioned us for this very purpose is God, who has given us the Spirit as a deposit, guaranteeing what is to come."*)

I need to be still and listen for His guidance. He will speak to me through various means, if I will only listen. Sometimes I have been gently nudged by the Holy Spirit. Sometimes I have been strongly warned. Sometimes I have listened; more often I am afraid I have not. So please, learn from my mistakes! You can trust God to guide you if you are only willing to let Him. You can trust your "gut instinct" when you are walking with the Lord.

There are times when it may feel as though you are just spinning your wheels, that God is giving you no direction at all. It may seem as if He is not listening. However, He is--ALWAYS. When you are not sure what you are to do, keep praying, and simply do what is immediately in front of you to do (even if that is as simple as washing your breakfast dishes or sweeping the floor), and continue to trust God to open the doors for you as He chooses. *Wait on the Lord!*

"For I know the plans I have for you," declares the Lord, *"plans to prosper you and not to harm you, plans to give you hope and a future."* (Jeremiah 29:11).

Live in the present with Him; refuse to worry about the future. *"Do not be anxious about anything, but in every situation, by prayer and petition, with thanksgiving, present your requests to God."* (Philippians 4:6)

Sometimes I have ignored the Holy Spirit's warning to my great detriment. My first marriage lasted nine years together, and two more separated. We separated when I was seven months pregnant with our second child. As described in an earlier chapter, my husband was carrying on an affair with another woman and told me he wanted to marry her. When our daughter Sara Elizabeth was born with a serious heart defect, I was living with my sister near Pittsburgh, and my husband was living in Cleveland. But shortly after my daughter Sara died in open heart surgery at age twenty-one months, my husband filed for divorce, and I did not contest it.

However, after my first husband's betrayal of trust, I was petrified at the thought of marrying again and the possibility of another betrayal. But I so desperately wanted to have another baby that I had gotten pregnant and miscarried several times in the thirteen years since my divorce. By this time I was in my early forties, and felt that I could not expect to carry another child full-term, given my history. Also, God had shown me after my last miscarriage that my compulsion to get pregnant even out of wedlock was based on a false sense of guilt for my two daughters being born with birth defects, but that this had not been my fault, nor under my control, and I needed to stop condemning myself for it. When I finally let go of this burden of guilt, I no longer needed to keep trying to get pregnant to prove to myself that I could "get it right this time" and carry a healthy baby. God showed me the roots of my compulsion were based in a false belief of guilt and self-condemnation, and so healed me of the need to continue my destructive behavior.

Then I met a man who had been divorced for several years, who had an eleven-year-old son living in foster care in another city. I thought this was surely my last chance to be a mother and to help raise a child. "Joe" (not his real name) went to my church; a mutual Christian friend had introduced us. Joe told me he had been an alcoholic, but he assured me that he was now a Christian and no longer drank. He attended my church every week, and we began dating. The warnings in my spirit were very strong against my getting involved with Joe, but I wanted so badly to be a mother! With his son having trouble in foster care in another city, it seemed that this was the perfect opportunity to rescue a child who was clearly in need of a lot of love, whose own mother had abandoned him at an early age. I decided to marry Joe so that we could take custody of his son, "Mike". We had been dating for only seven months.

Despite the alarm bells sounding loudly in my spirit, we went down to the New York City courthouse one warm spring day in May, and were married. We then headed to upstate New York for a short weekend honeymoon. As we drove out of the city in our rental car, I was overcome with a sense of dread. I had the strongest desire to simply turn around right then and there, and declare it all a mistake! However, I set my jaw and went ahead, determined to continue what I had started, in spite of my gut feelings. After a brief honeymoon, Joe and I returned to New York City. We found a large two-bedroom apartment in the same neighborhood where I had been living in my one-bedroom apartment before our marriage. We then took custody of his son.

Things were difficult from the start. Joe's son had severe psychological problems from a mother who had neglected and abused him, and a father who had been absent. Mike was jealous of me, and wanted his Dad to get back together with his real Mom, fantasizing that then she would want him back as well. He acted out, stole things from me, and generally was always getting into trouble.

Trying to help him, I persuaded a private Christian school in the neighborhood to accept him, even though he was far behind his grade level. I hoped that the new school environment could turn Mike around, and that it would keep him away from the bad influences at the local public school in our northern Manhattan neighborhood. But soon the neighborhood kids were telling me that Mike was drinking beer, stealing hood ornaments from cars, and setting fires in trash cans, among other things. I had no idea how to handle this child (whom a psychiatrist later told us was sociopathic). My husband tried to be Mike's buddy rather than discipline him. We went to family counseling but nothing seemed to help.

In a desperate attempt to give my stepson a better environment, we moved to Manassas, Virginia, away from New York City's rough neighborhoods and temptations. But things did not improve. Not only did my stepson continue to find bad company to hang out with to drink and do drugs, but my husband couldn't seem to find a job, and was content to stay at home all day while I went off to work. My job as a legal secretary in Washington, D.C. meant commuting an hour and a half each way, and I was gone for twelve hours a day. I also found out later that Joe was secretly drinking at home, and my stepson, with no adult supervision, was hanging out with friends after school, getting high on anything he could find. One time when he was around thirteen years old, Mike accidentally set fire to a truck full of hay when he and a friend were hiding out in the back of the truck smoking marijuana. Our household was in constant turmoil. I never knew what I would find when I got home each evening.

The Holy Spirit had tried to warn me several times not to get into this situation, but in my blind stubbornness to become a mother in any way I could, I had ignored all the warnings in my spirit. I tried to stick it out, despite the deepening problems in our marriage. For the next four years, we lived in northern Virginia, and we tried through several counselors to get help for my stepson, who eventually ended up in a juvenile residential treatment facility. My husband wanted to help his son, but he didn't know how. He continued to drink secretly. Joe had a ferocious temper when he drank. Early on in our marriage I was unafraid of Joe, and I quickly stepped between Joe and his son on those rare occasions when he got so angry at Mike that he would try to hit him with his fists (Joe was well over six feet and solidly built). Immediately I would stop Joe, certain that he would never dare to hit me.

But a few years into our marriage, there came a night when Mike did not come home after school. We were frantic with worry looking for him. He finally showed up around nine p.m. When he refused to tell us where he had been, Joe went after Mike and slammed him against the wall and started punching him in the face. I suddenly realized that this time I was afraid to step between them, that I thought Joe in his fury might pummel me as well. I yelled at him to stop, but I did not physically try to stop him. Instead I called the police to come and stop the fight. They took Joe to the jail overnight. My stepson was not hurt and stayed at home with me. But I was badly shaken. Even though Joe had never yet hit me or physically come after me, I realized I no longer felt safe, and that I was afraid of him.

It shocked me to realize that over the space of four years I had allowed Joe to gradually steal a part of my sense of self and my identity. I had always had a strong sense of self and thought I would never allow myself to be treated that way. I knew I had to leave. It took me nearly twelve more months to do that, however, and to be entirely certain that this was what I should do. It did not help that the elders at the church we belonged to in Virginia tried to convince me to stay, not fully understanding the danger I was in. They wanted to believe Joe's assurances of better behavior in the future. But they did not know that Joe continued to drink heavily in secret. I often came home from my Saturday morning choir practice to find him sleeping off a drinking binge (I was naive about alcoholism, and for quite a while just thought he liked to sleep a lot, but later found out he was drinking when I wasn't home).

In retrospect, I am glad that I already knew Jesus personally and was so strongly aware of His love for me. If Jesus had not been so close to me in my prayer time and guiding me, that particular church's actions to excommunicate me when I left Joe could have soured me on "patriarchal religion" altogether, and I may have turned away from church fellowship permanently. (As it was, it made me less trusting of the next church "family" that I became a part of.) As I prayed and sought out God's guidance, however, He made it very clear to me that I needed to leave Joe, both for my mental health and my physical safety. I made plans to leave.

A few days after I told Joe that I was going to look for an apartment and move out, I had one of the biggest scares of my life. It was about 7:30 a.m. on a weekday morning, and we were both getting ready to go to work. (My stepson Mike, now sixteen, was in a residential treatment center and no longer lived with us.) I casually walked into the kitchen where Joe was preparing his lunch sandwiches.

Suddenly, in a robotic voice with no emotion, Joe said to me: "God told me to put my hands around your neck and squeeze until you were dead."

I was in shock at what he said and the strange unnatural way his voice sounded. I quickly turned around and hurried back to the bathroom and locked myself in. I had no idea what to do. I prayed to God for help, not knowing if it was safe to come out of the bathroom.

After some minutes of silence, I opened the door of the bathroom and walked the few feet down the narrow hallway in our small two-bedroom apartment towards the kitchen, being careful to stand in the dining area several feet away from Joe in case I had to run. I asked him if he meant what he had said a few minutes before. He replied in his normal voice, "Kathy, you are not safe here. You should leave."

I knew then that this was God's answer to my prayer, since Joe had said this in his normal voice, and with authority. I went back to the bathroom and locked the door again, waiting for him to leave for work. He did not say anything more nor try to get me to come out of the bathroom.

When I heard him go out the door of the apartment, I quickly packed a suitcase, taking it with me on the train into Washington, D.C., where I worked as a legal secretary at a large law firm. Still fearful, I told the receptionist at the firm to not allow my husband to get past her desk, and to call security if he came in. I also advised my supervisor in the Human Resources Department about what was happening in case he showed up.

That evening, I did not go back to our apartment, but instead went to a motel to stay for a couple of days. After that I stayed at a friend's house for a few weeks. She and her husband welcomed me, and invited me to stay there as long as I needed. They did not let Joe know where I was.

I never went alone to our apartment to see Joe again. Friends came with me to pick up my things once I had found a safe place to live in Washington D.C., close to where I worked. For several months after that, I was afraid that Joe might come after me at my new apartment building in downtown D.C., even though it had a doorman and good security. I paid close attention to where I walked and avoided unlit areas and deserted streets at night. Although I knew I could depend on God's protection, Joe's strange behavior and threatening words had shaken me more deeply than I was willing to admit. It took me several months before I was no longer afraid that he might suddenly jump out from a dark street corner whenever I had to walk outside of my building at night.

Despite these natural fears, through my whole marriage to Joe and through all of these events, I knew I had God's protection. Jesus did not leave me even when I disobeyed His warnings and married Joe. **Jesus never left me!** He gave me many words of comfort in that time when I turned to Him, and He directed my steps. But because I had chosen a path that the Holy Spirit had so strongly warned me against when I married Joe, I found myself fighting demons for those five years that I did not know how to fight, and I was bruised badly in the battle.

Praise God for His mercy! He rescued me from the pit that I had dug for myself! Although I came out muddy and scarred, His light was stronger in me, for I had learned to cling more tightly to Him through those difficult times. This is my cautionary tale, dear friends. Listen to the Holy Spirit when He speaks to you. Listen to your "gut" instincts! Sometimes God warns us through them!

The Lord in His great love for us sends us help in many ways: through the advice of good friends (<u>all</u> of whom had warned me <u>not</u> to marry Joe), through various circumstances, or through a particular event unique to your situation. Do not be as stubborn and wayward as I was when I did not heed His warnings. God did not want a bad marriage for me, but the Holy Spirit does not force us to do what is good for us. He will nudge us, warn us, even speak to our hearts. But if we still choose to go our own way, He will let us do so.

Now when I sense He is speaking to me, I know I need to listen. I need daily time in His Word and in prayer in order to hear His voice. I have learned to pay closer attention to that "still, small voice", that intuition, or gut instinct as I sometimes call it. **Jesus is always your best friend!** Like any human relationship, the more you get to know Him, the easier it is to recognize His voice and to know His character. That is why it is so important to set aside the time every day to read the Bible and to pray, and *listen*.

God knows our weaknesses before we do, and if, or rather <u>when</u> we wander off, He never condemns us when we return to Him. He forgives us even before we ask, and welcomes us into His loving arms once again. A good illustration of this is in the parable of the Prodigal Son, and the picture of the father who runs out to embrace his returning son before the son even has a chance to ask his father's forgiveness! (Luke 15:20)

As Jesus told Peter when Peter asked how many times he should forgive someone – up to seven times? No, Jesus said, seventy times seven! There is no limit to how many times we are to forgive another, and there is no limit to how many times God will forgive us, if we are only sorry for our sin and ask.

Dear friend, ask! The Holy Spirit lives within you if you have received Jesus Christ as your Savior. His work is to be your Advocate, and to reveal Christ to you. Ask for guidance, for everything you need in this life. **God loves you so much! You are His child and He will "guide you with His eye".**

"I will instruct you and teach you in the way you should go; I will guide you with My eye." (Psalm 32:8)

CHAPTER ELEVEN

MORE SURPRISES! GOD'S GIFTS.

*"May he give you the desire of your heart
and make all your plans succeed."* (Psalm 20:4)

After living for a year in Washington, D.C., I moved back to New York City. This was still my favorite place to live, and I had many good friends there, despite having been away for five years. I was newly divorced, and single again after two failed marriages. A lot of water under the bridge as they say, and some of it pretty dirty. *Thank God that His mercies are new every morning!*

I quickly found a permanent legal secretarial job at a big law firm down near Battery Park, the same Wall Street firm where I had frequently "temped" when I was living in the city a few years before. After a few weeks of staying with a friend, I found the perfect one-bedroom apartment in a grand old building on a lovely, quiet street on the Upper West Side in Manhattan, not far from Columbia University. I was only steps away from St. John's Cathedral, whose bells delightfully chimed each hour during the daytime.

I decided to return to Redeemer Church, since I had enjoyed Dr. Tim Keller's preaching so much when I last lived in the city. The church had grown from about a hundred people to well over two thousand people in the five years I had been away. They now held multiple services each Sunday, the largest at Hunter College auditorium on the East Side, but also afternoon and evening services on the West Side of Manhattan. In addition, there were several home Bible studies held in Manhattan, depending on which neighborhood you lived in.

Since I lived on the Upper West Side, the home Bible study closest to me was about ten blocks down the street, in the west 90's. The couple who held the study had two small children. The husband was often out of town on business, though, and his wife, Elizabeth, was the actual study leader. We would start with singing, led by a young woman with a guitar. We then spent time reading and discussing a particular Bible passage, closed with prayer, and had light refreshments. There were ordinarily six or seven of us there besides the Bible study leader, and most were still in college or just starting out in their careers. I was one of the oldest there.

One evening, a new person arrived to join the group. Daniel was very tall (6'7"), handsome, well-groomed, wearing gold-framed glasses, dark pants, a finely pressed white shirt and tie. His dark hair was swept back from his high forehead with just a touch of silver at the temples. He was clearly well-educated, intelligent and articulate. When we prayed, he spoke with care, and his deep voice had authority. I could sense in my spirit from the way he prayed that he had a strong relationship with the Lord.

Afterwards, we got better acquainted as we munched on cookies and drank ginger ale. I learned that he loved the pipe organ and the music of J.S. Bach. This especially impressed me, since Johann Sebastian Bach is my all-time favorite composer! He also told me he had wanted to be an opera singer in college, but was now working as a computer consultant. His clear love of God, his intellect, and our mutual interests attracted me from the start.

As I got ready to leave to walk the ten blocks back to my apartment alone, I discovered Daniel also planned to walk in the same direction. He lived on Riverside Drive and 110th Street, only a few blocks from my apartment on 111th Street near Amsterdam Avenue. We walked together, continuing our conversation. Soon we had established a habit of walking home together after the Bible study each week. At other times we would meet just for conversation and coffee in the neighborhood, enjoying each other's company.

A few months later, I took a new evening legal secretarial job so that I could practice the organ more during the weekdays for my church job on Sunday, and also practice the flute more. This meant, however, that I could no longer attend the weekday evening Bible study. Although Daniel and I still met sometimes for coffee and remained friends, we did not spend much time together, since I was dating an old flame whom I was still in love with, and hoped to marry.

Then Daniel had to leave the city and return to Memphis to take care of his mother, who was dying of ovarian cancer. He was an only child, and felt keenly his responsibility to be there by her side. We spoke occasionally by telephone, but I did not see him for more than a year. When his mother died, he stayed in Memphis to take care of her estate.

Then several things happened at once. First, I broke up with the man I had been so in love with, discovering he had lied to me all along, and not only never intended to marry me, but had continued seeing other women without my knowing. It was the week before Thanksgiving, and it was also the first Thanksgiving after 9/11. Everyone in New York City walked around in shock in the days following that terrible attack, and it seemed that even in this last week of November we were still suffering from the traumatic psychological effects. How well I remember walking by Rockefeller Center at Fifth Avenue and 51st Street barely a week after 9/11, looking up at those magnificent buildings, and asking myself if they would be hit next. I had not known personally anyone who died at The World Trade Center, but I had friends and work colleagues who had lost loved ones. The mood in the city was very subdued, even as holiday decorations went up as usual on every street.

Having also just broken up with my supposed fiancé, I was feeling pretty low. Then Daniel arrived in the city with Thanksgiving plans, and called to ask me to dinner. He was staying in the Hilton in midtown Manhattan, a very large hotel with several fine restaurants. We met for dinner at the hotel's most elegant restaurant. We sat opposite each other in a very romantic environment of soft lighting, white linen tablecloths and delicious food, with a well-dressed waiter standing discreetly nearby. I said to Daniel, "This feels like a date!"

He said, "Do you want it to be?"

I said, "Oh, no, we are just friends!"

Still, there was something different in the air, a hint of romance alongside our comfortable friendship. I went home and did not dwell on it, as Daniel was leaving the next day.

The following Wednesday after Thanksgiving, I was at home in my apartment in Manhattan, playing flute and clarinet duets with a good friend. The doorbell rang and a deliveryman handed me a large bouquet of a dozen long-stemmed red roses. I was rather startled, and as I read the card with it, I was puzzled as well. The card merely said, *"love, Daniel".* I told my friend Kim that this was very confusing, as Daniel and I were just friends, and I did not understand why he was sending me a dozen red roses. She had no answer for it either. Later that evening, I e-mailed Daniel a simple thank you note for the flowers, without saying more.

The next day I received a letter in the mail, and after reading it, I suddenly understood the flowers! Daniel had written me a long heartfelt letter, explaining his deepening feelings for me, and how he hoped that I might be open to building a closer relationship. The flowers had mistakenly been delivered early; he had ordered them to arrive on the next day, thinking that I would get them after I had read the letter. I was completely surprised! I did not feel these same feelings he was now expressing towards me. In fact, since it was only two weeks before that I had broken up with this other man who had lied to me and betrayed me, I was convinced I should not let any man into my life very soon.

Two days before this, I had even sent out my annual Christmas letter early, telling everyone that since I had obviously done such a poor job of choosing men in my life in the past, that this time I was determined to let God pick out the next man for me! Little did I know that the Lord had been waiting for me to let go of the man I had so mistakenly chosen, and He had the man <u>He</u> had chosen waiting in the wings for me all along!

After a day or two of pondering how to answer him, I wrote Daniel a long letter back, explaining that I did not have romantic feelings for him and was interested only in friendship for now. However, I said that I was willing to consider the possibility of a deeper relationship developing in the future. He later told me how he read that letter in disappointment, but told himself, "Well, she didn't say no!"

In sharing my letter with a married couple who were his best friends in Memphis, they also said, "She didn't say no!" They told him he should fly up to New York again to see me.

So Daniel made plans to surprise me with a visit to New York the weekend after Christmas. Fortunately for him, his friends told him he had better let me know that he was coming, as I might have other plans. In fact, I had planned to go with several girlfriends to see the movie "Beautiful Mind" that Friday evening, and on Sunday, after playing organ at my church job, I planned to meet another female friend for lunch, and then attend a small opera performance in the afternoon in which a male friend of mine had a part. After the opera, I had planned to go out to dinner with this friend and others on Sunday evening. So when Daniel called, I told him that I was only free on Saturday to spend time with him. I knew he planned to stay again at the same Hilton in mid-town Manhattan, as he had sold his condo on the Upper West Side by that time.

On Friday evening, after seeing the movie, I was chatting happily with my friends as the four of us approached the steps of the building where I lived on West 111th Street. I looked up, and there stood Daniel at the entrance of my building. He was very attractive standing there: tall, handsome, and imposing in his long grey wool overcoat, dress pants, and perfectly shined shoes. My girlfriends were impressed! I was surprised to see him, but introduced him to the two friends he did not know (he knew my friend Maureen already), and after a few minutes' conversation, my friends went on to their respective homes.

I invited Daniel to come up to my apartment. (He had never been in my apartment, since when he had lived in Manhattan, we had always met at the neighborhood coffee shop, or at the Bible study leader's house.) It was a very small one-bedroom apartment--in anywhere but Manhattan, it would have been called a studio apartment. The narrow living room was modestly furnished, with a green IKEA futon couch that doubled as a bed for out-of-town visitors, a small TV and stereo on a black metal two-shelved stand, a wooden side chair, an IKEA light pine coffee table, and two tall floor lamps. Daniel sat down on one end of the couch, and I sat down on the other, leaving a good amount of space between us. I offered him some tea or coffee, which he declined.

Daniel told me he had flown in earlier that day. He said he couldn't wait to see me and talk to me, so he had decided to come up to my neighborhood (his old neighborhood as well), hoping to catch me when I got home from the movies. After sharing recent news, Daniel told me that he believed God was leading us to be together. He had flown up that weekend to ask me to marry him. We had not even kissed or held hands up to this point! I could not believe what I was hearing! I opened my mouth in astonishment.

I told Daniel that it would be a long time before I could know if that was the right thing for me to do, and that we would need to date for several months at least before I could answer such a question. He understood my reluctance. He simply told me that he would not have asked me so soon, except that he had felt strongly led by the Holy Spirit to ask me now. I laughed, but in astonishment and without making fun of him, because I knew he had a deep prayer life and loved the Lord. I simply repeated that it would take me time to know him better, and to get over my previous broken relationship. We made plans to meet the next day (Saturday), for dinner and an evening out.

When I arrived to meet Daniel at the Hilton Hotel the next afternoon around 5 p.m., he greeted me with a single long-stemmed red rose. It was a blustery cold wintry day in December, with no flowers blooming outside, and it touched me that he had a rose for me. We went on to dinner at a small romantic Italian restaurant in midtown. Daniel was definitely pulling out all the stops for me--there was even a violinist who came around to the tables to play song requests. We had strong red wine, delicious lasagna, sweet tiramisus and cappuccinos as we lingered over our dinner, sharing more fully than ever before the stories of our lives, our hopes and our dreams.

We wound up the evening at a popular local jazz club in mid-town, where we sat closely together in a dimly-lit room packed full of people. We now held hands for the first time. The gruff throaty sounds of the tenor saxophone and the brilliant improvisations of the piano player were still playing in my head afterwards as I rode the subway home alone to my apartment. It had been the perfect romantic evening! I was sorry that I could not spend Sunday with Daniel because of my previously scheduled plans. However, I told Daniel I could see him on Monday (New Year's Eve day). He planned to stay until New Year's Day in the city before flying back to Memphis.

The next day, I played for church as planned, and met my girlfriend for lunch, and then I went on to the opera alone to see my singer friend perform. But my thoughts were constantly on Daniel. I knew I was being wooed by him, and it was having its effect! As I listened to the arias from the opera "The Magic Flute" by Mozart, I could not help thinking that God had arranged this, since the whole opera seemed to be about the delights of marriage. As the poor man Papageno sang to lovely Papagena, courting her and trying to win her love, I could think only of Daniel. After the opera, I decided to go home, rather than go out to dinner with my friend. Since he had several other friends there too and they were all going out to dinner together, I did not feel too badly leaving him immediately after congratulating him on his performance in the opera. I had been out all day in the city, and was more than ready to get back home.

Arriving back at my apartment around seven-thirty p.m., I immediately called Daniel and explained that I was home early, and that he could come up to see me if he wished. He caught a taxicab and arrived twenty minutes later. I confessed to him that I could not get him off my mind all day, and had decided to come home sooner than I had originally planned so that we could see each other. He then told me that he had been praying and fasting all that day. After going to church in the morning, he had specifically asked God that if I was the woman he was to marry, that God would ensure that I would not be able to get him off my mind all day, and that I would call him and want to see him that evening. God had certainly fulfilled his request!

We now sat closer together on the couch; I was feeling much more comfortable with him. My admiration for him and my deepening attraction to him were obvious to me as he talked about his plans for his ministry. He was now on his first assignment as a supply pastor for two churches on the outskirts of Memphis. This was only his second assignment as a minister, since he had been a computer consultant when living in Manhattan, and had completed seminary only a couple of years earlier. When I met him at the Bible study, he had just begun serving in his first position as an interim pastor for a church in New Jersey, just across the bridge from Manhattan. But when his mother got so sick, he had needed to suddenly move to Memphis to take care of her, and so had to leave all of that behind. After his mother died, he had decided to stay in Memphis as he cleared up her estate, and he had found work there.

Before he left for the evening, he again asked me to marry him. We now kissed for the first time. But I still said no. It was all too soon, and happening way too fast for me. I felt sure that I would need months before I could know the answer to that question. Daniel left disappointed, but we made plans to meet the very next day (Monday, December 31st, 2001).

The next morning I talked with Jesus during my devotional time about the whole matter. It was amazing to me how strong my feelings had become for Daniel in such a short time. I knew I was falling in love with him, but still it all seemed to be happening so fast. Suddenly I heard in my spirit a quiet voice saying: *"What are you waiting for? This is right. Go ahead."* I knew it was the Lord speaking.

I called Daniel and said, "Ask me again."

He understood immediately what I meant. He said: "Will you marry me?"

I said, "Yes."

Yes!! I was smiling like crazy on my end of the phone, full of joy! I knew Daniel on the other end of the phone felt that same happiness.

Daniel asked me to meet him at Tiffany's on 57th Street in Manhattan to pick out an engagement ring. I rushed out the door in my ski sweater and jeans, not even taking the time to put on any makeup! I was too excited. It all seemed like a fairy tale come true. I realized that God had been waiting to bless me with this man, Daniel, whom I had known as a friend for over two years, but had never considered as possibly more than that in all that time.

God had patiently waited until I was ready to listen to Him, and no longer blinded by my old feelings for the man who had charmed me years before, but had never been truthful with me. Daniel was the opposite of that crafty man: Daniel spoke the truth plainly and did not sugarcoat things. In fact, he had told me that that I was wrong to be with the other man (who was not a

Christian) soon after he met me, even when other friends did not try to dissuade me from what they saw as a hopeless case.

Soon I was standing next to Daniel at Tiffany's glass-enclosed diamond cases, picking out my beautiful sparkling diamond engagement ring. We then went out to lunch. We walked along the street hand in hand. We couldn't stop smiling. After lunch, I called my mother and told her about Daniel and my sudden engagement (my father had died the previous summer). She was very surprised, but happy for me too. We set a date to be married the weekend after Valentine's Day at the little church in Pennsylvania where I had grown up. This meant we had only about six weeks to get everything ready. Daniel flew back to Memphis to prepare his house there, while I arranged to end the lease early on my apartment and to pack up all my stuff. I also had to wrap up my church position in Manhattan. We planned to live in Memphis for the foreseeable future.

Two weeks later, Daniel flew back to New York, and we drove over together to Pennsylvania so that my family could meet him for the first time. My mother and siblings were anxious to get to know him. They all liked him immediately, and shared in my happiness as we told the story of our whirlwind courtship.

Our wedding day arrived (February 16, 2002). Suddenly at the last minute, amidst all the excitement, I had an anxiety attack. What was I doing?? Here I was, promising to be with this man for the rest of my life, when we had only been engaged for a few weeks, and most of that time we had been apart (he in Tennessee, me in New York). Fifteen minutes before I was to walk down the aisle, and suddenly I was feeling so uncertain and afraid! But then I thought of those words from Jesus, and I gained strength: *"This is right. Go ahead."*

As the organist played Purcell's Trumpet Voluntary, I walked down the church aisle. I was almost ready to cry in my nervousness, but nevertheless I was certain that it was God's plan for me to marry this man who also loved the Lord. We were joined in purpose: to love God and to love each other.

I reached the front of the church where Daniel stood waiting, tall and strong. As the congregation sang the first hymn, I turned to Daniel, looked up at him, and smiled with happiness, knowing: *"This is right. Go ahead."*

****

"For this reason a man shall leave his father and mother and be joined to his wife, and the two shall become one flesh; so then they are no longer two, but one flesh." (Mark 10:7-8)

Judy, Mom and me 1947

West Virginia University 1968

**Sara and I Getting Acquainted,
July 1977**

Sara and me, Christmas 1977

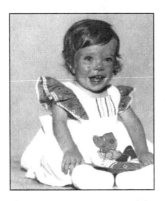

Sara Elizabeth, One Year Old 1978

Sara Elizabeth, 19 Months Old 1979

Mom and Dad at Home, circa 1980s

Dad and me, circa 1980s

**Mom, Kathy, Jack, Sue, Doug, Judy, Fay,
circa 1990**

Me with flute, 2002

Mom and me, Wedding Day Feb. 16, 2002

Daniel, me, Pastor Mark—Wedding Vows

Daniel and me, Wedding Day Feb. 16, 2002

PART II:
REFLECTIONS

CHAPTER TWELVE

LOVE IS KEY

"Dear friends, let us love one another, for love comes from God...
Whoever does not love does not know God, because God is love.
(I John 4:7-8)

*L*ove is key. This is surely the most important thing we can learn from God, *for He is Love.* Love one another! Help me love, Lord! Help me forgive--because love requires forgiveness. This is both the first thing and the last thing we should learn. Love one another! For without love we are like *"sounding brass or clashing cymbals"* (*see* I Cor. 13:1).

Looking back, I see how very fortunate I was to have parents who always loved me. There are many stories I could tell of my mother's sacrificial love, but here are two of my favorites, which illustrate her character.

I was seventeen when I got my driver's license. With my new independence, I impulsively decided to "borrow" my mother's car to go visit my boyfriend, who lived about twelve miles away (in the small town of Clarion, PA). After crossing the bridge over the Clarion River on Route 322, there is a long steep curving hill going up into the town. My mother's car, an old dark blue four-door Ford sedan, was at that stage where the engine burned through a quart of oil as if it were a teaspoon. In my adolescent ignorance, I paid no attention to the sudden clanking and clattering noises I heard from the engine as I drove up the long hill. Suddenly the car came to a dead stop just halfway up the hill. Apparently the oil had all burned up and the piston rods had overheated, destroying the engine. I was responsible for destroying my mother's only means of transportation to her job! Not only had my poor mother not given me permission to take her car, but now she was about to learn she had no car, and had to find both a way to come get me and to arrange to get the car towed. I walked on up the hill to the gas station located on the opposite side of the road close to town and called her. She had every right to yell at me, and to berate me for my foolishness. But she heard my sorrow over what I had done, accepted my tearful apology, and forgave me. She never brought it up again, even though it caused her a lot of difficulty and expense which she could not well afford (since she had to buy a new car at a time when just keeping food on the table was a struggle).

Another favorite story is about the time when I was nearing the end of my freshman year at college (West Virginia University, which I attended on scholarship and student loans). Even though I was a college music major with flute as my major instrument, I did not yet own a flute. The flute I was using belonged to my high school band department. Mr. Klahr Peterson, my dearly beloved band director, had first handed me a flute in the fifth grade. He had given me my first and only lessons until I started college, and had allowed me to take a school-owned flute with me to college for that first year (since I could not afford to buy one).

My college flute teacher had just received a new professional flute (made by the Haynes company in Boston) which was for another student, but that student had cancelled her order at the last minute. Haynes flutes at that time (1965) were so popular that they had to be back-ordered, and people waited for several months to get their hand-crafted instrument. My teacher knew

I had only an old student model instrument, cheaply made, and suggested that I should buy this flute while it was still available.

I called my Mom and told her I needed to buy this flute now. It was around $700, a large amount of money in 1965, and a seemingly impossible amount for my mother and father, who both worked very hard but had no extra money. My mother, however, was determined to help me get the flute of my dreams. Even though it was already early on a Friday evening, she went to the local small-town bank, which at that time stayed open late on Fridays for the convenience of its customers, and persuaded the bank manager to loan her the money so that I could buy the flute. (My teacher had graciously advanced her own money to pay for the flute and was holding it for me while I contacted my parents.)

I do not know how long it took my mother to pay off that loan, but it couldn't have been easy for her, since we were poor and every penny was needed. She never mentioned her sacrifice, however. Nor did she ever hold her sacrifice over me as if I owed her something in return. She was simply delighted that I could finally have my own flute, knowing how much it meant to me.

I played that same Haynes flute for the next twenty-five years. A flute from the "golden era" of Haynes flute manufacturing, it had a beautiful warm tone, and I received many compliments from playing it. How fortunate I was! God had given me one of the most precious gifts a child can receive--a mother's sacrificial love. Mom had gladly given up her own needs to help me succeed.

Do you know how much you are loved by God? He loves us **so much more** than we can understand. Trust His love. He will never mislead or fail you! **Never!!** We may not understand why He is allowing something hard in our lives, but we will "understand it better by and by", as the beloved spiritual says.

Love comes in so many ways, both small actions and large.It is seen in a thousand ways which need no explanation. Did the city policeman have to buy a pair of boots for the homeless man? Did Danny Thomas have to establish St Jude Hospital for children with cancer? Acts of love are almost always easy to recognize, although "tough love" may not always be understood as love, especially if it is for one's ultimate good, but denies a present gratification. But even God tells us that He *"disciplines those whom He loves"* (Hebrews 12:6).

How have I shown love today? *Have* I shown love today? How *can* I show love today? My neighbor, my friend, my co-worker, my family members--do they see love in me? Do they see *Jesus* in me? *"For God is love, and he who loves is of God"* (I John 4:7-8).

> *"As the Father has loved me, so have I loved you. Now remain in my love. If you keep my commands, you will remain in my love, just as I have kept my Father's commands and remain in his love. I have told you this so that my joy may be in you and that your joy may be complete. My command is this: Love each other as I have loved you.* (John 15:9-12)

CHAPTER THIRTEEN

PRAISE GOD CONTINUALLY

"Rejoice in the Lord always; and again I say, Rejoice."
(Philippians 4:4)

*T*ake a walk. I mean it! (Right after you read this chapter <smile>!) I don't know about you, but often I find myself complaining to God more than thanking Him. Through my clouded vision I see the glass as half-empty, not half-full. But if I go outside and observe His creation, I am moved to praise Him for the wonder and glory that I see. Whether it is a chirping bird or a grasshopper jumping through the grass, colorful summer flowers or a pure white winter snow, a gray dawn or a rose-colored sunset, God's work is always a wonder to behold. It moves my heart to praise Him, and it takes my eyes off of myself. On a walk my vision clears, and I can see Him through the work of His creation more easily. It is akin to when you see the workmanship of a fine piece of furniture, and in so doing then admire the skill of the carpenter who made it. Likewise, when I observe what He has made, I am grateful to the Master Carpenter. This is how we are made: to praise Him and enjoy His presence forever!

I once read that Corrie Ten Boom and her sister even praised God for the cockroaches in their sleeping quarters at a Nazi prison camp during World War II, because the cockroaches meant the prison guards did not want to come into their quarters, and they were able to hold their Bible studies undisturbed. What an incredible faith, and what an inspiration for us to strive to have that kind of thankful attitude in even the most horrific of circumstances. As the Apostle Paul said, *"I have learned to be content whatever the circumstances"* (Philippians 4:11).

The key to happiness in our walk with God is surely praise. *"In everything give thanks"* (I Thessalonians 5:18). We can praise Him *in the midst of* everything, knowing that even in the bad things that happen to us, God will mysteriously and miraculously use them for our good. *"All things work together for good for those that love God and are called according to His purpose"* (Romans 8:28).

We cannot understand this mystery, but we can trust God by faith, since we know He is faithful. He fulfills His Word, and He is always true to His Word. When we choose to offer Him a sacrifice of praise even when we least feel like it, we will find our spirits renewed and our hearts lifted up to worship in His presence.

This is His desire for us: first, to know Him and to experience His love, and second, to share that love with others. We can find that peace that passes understanding, that joy in Him in the midst of our pain, when we seek Him first, and praise Him in obedience to His will. Praise Him even when you don't feel like it! In fact, we especially need to praise Him when we don't feel like it, so that God can soften our hearts and lift us up to joy in the heavenly places.

Lift our eyes above and look at Him. He is always worthy of our praise! Look at His character, His holiness, His righteousness, His perfection. Meditate on His love for us, so great that He came down from heaven to die for us and to give us eternal life. If we will praise God with our whole heart, we will be filled with His joy, and our circumstances will no longer bind us. For we see that with God, all things truly are possible.

Praising God in every moment does not mean that we will never be sad! We will still feel the grief of losing a loved one when that person dies. We will still weep over the evil done on this earth. There are times when tears and grief are the only fitting response to what has happened. Jesus shows us this when He weeps at Lazarus' tomb, *even when He knew that He would shortly raise him from the dead.* He still wept for the pain and sorrow already endured, and the separation of loved ones from one another.

Praising Him does mean, however, that the Lord will <u>lift you up</u> and that you can sense His love in your spirit, even when you are sorrowful. It means, too, that the heaviness of heart and the burdens that you carry will be lightened. He wishes to carry our burdens for us. *"Come **unto me**, all ye that labour and are heavy laden, and I will give you rest."* (Matthew 11:28) (KJV)

As the author Sarah Young describes in words she attributes to Jesus: *"It is impossible to spend too much time thanking and praising Me. I created you first and foremost to glorify Me. Thanksgiving and praise put you in proper relationship with Me, opening the way for My riches to flow into you. As you thank Me for My Presence and Peace, you appropriate My richest gifts."* (<u>Jesus Calling</u>, p. 340).

Sometimes we don't feel like praising God because we are angry with Him or in rebellion. This is the most important time to go to Him. Pour out your heart to Him! He already knows you completely, so nothing you can say will shock Him. He has seen the things you have tried to keep hidden; He knows your every thought.

After you have that honest conversation with Him, begin praising Him. Praise Him for whatever you see for which you can praise Him, even the smallest thing. It may be simply that you are alive today and able to breathe. It may be for your family. It may be for the things He has created – the sun, moon, stars, grass, trees, a singing bird, etc. Whatever comes to mind for which you can honestly praise Him, that is the place to start. Even if you <u>feel</u> no joy in anything, simply praise Him for sending Jesus to die for you, and for giving you salvation, for it is the greatest gift of all.

Even when we feel nothing, we can praise Him with our will. I recently was surprised as I got ready to go and direct a choir rehearsal at my church, that I seemed to feel nothing. It was as though my emotions were flat-lined, even though working with the choir usually gave me great joy. Then the next day, I discovered that I was allergic to the Bactrim antibiotic I had been taking for several days for a sinus infection, and that one of the allergic reactions is to no longer feel any emotion. This was the first time medication had affected me like that. As soon as I stopped the medication, my emotions returned to normal. I mention this incident because sometimes we may not know why our feelings are "dead", but we can still choose to praise God. Even when we feel nothing, God is pleased when we offer Him the "sacrifice of praise". Eventually our emotions will line up with our will, and we will feel that joy again if we will only persist in thanking God in every circumstance. A quiet stillness or an exuberant dancing about, both are acceptable sacrifices of praise and pleasing to God, who sees the heart.

Praise Him! Time and time again He has lifted me up out of discouragement or depression. He can do the same for you. *"Turn your eyes upon Jesus, look full in His wonderful face – and the things of earth will grow strangely dim, in the light of His wonder and grace."* ("Turn Your Eyes upon Jesus", hymn written by Helen Lemmel).

God will never give you more than you can bear. When my obstetrician came into my hospital room the day after my second daughter was born and told me that they were sending her to Children's Hospital of Pittsburgh because something was clearly wrong, although they were not sure what it was yet, I cried out, "No, I can't bear it if this child dies too" (since my first daughter had died at age two months).

But my doctor answered, "God won't give you more than you can bear." *(see* I Cor. 10:13).

I said, "That can't be true. This would be more than I can bear."

However, in the next months, I discovered it was true. **God will give you the grace to handle whatever He puts in your life.** He gave me the faith and strength to trust Him through everything that happened during that time. When my daughter Sara died in open heart surgery at age twenty-one months, He led me directly to His beautiful words of comfort and peace in Psalm 139:16: *"all of your days were numbered, before one of them came to be".*

In the months after Sara's death, He showed me that the only way out of that deep pit of grief over my loss was to praise Him for the gift of her life, and to be thankful for the precious time I had been given with her. I learned to thank Him for the gift I had received in mothering her for twenty-one months, instead of focusing on what I did not have.

This doesn't mean that I don't still miss her, and excitedly look forward to the day when I will see her again in heaven. However, by learning to be thankful for the time I had with her and to be grateful for that time, it brought me up out of that dark pit of paralyzing grief (and still does today many years later).

It may sound strange to say this, but I have discovered that when I can let go and think unselfishly about it, I am thankful that my daughters have been raised in heaven, and so have not had to face sin and the consequences of sin in this life. What a gift! I know that they are safely in heaven. It helps me to realize that, although I feel the loss of not raising them on earth and seeing them grow up, their gain is greater, as they are in heaven and raised in perfection, and I can rejoice in that. I trust God knew what is best for them and for me. He sees the future while we can't, and I trust His purposes in allowing this present separation. And, in a short span of time, I will be with them for all of eternity.

There is so much to be thankful for, no matter how hard your present circumstances may be. We have an eternal home, an eternal hope in heaven, by God's unmerited gift of love.

When I praise God in the worst of times, I consistently find that He lifts me up, and I am no longer caught in my self-pity. Instead, I am given a new perspective. He strengthens me and gives me joy in Him, and deep gratitude for the active work of His Spirit in my life.

The only way to be content in every circumstance is to keep your eyes fixed on Jesus.

A Prayer of Thanksgiving

Praise You, God!
Praise You for Who You Are;
Thank You for saving me from my sins;
for giving me eternal life;
for the beauty of Your creation;
for the wonders of Your love;
for Your constant protection;
for Your faithfulness;
for Your peace that passes understanding.

Praise You, God!
For Your omniscience;
for Your foreknowledge;
Thank You for choosing me to be Yours forever;
for the promise of heaven and eternal joy;
for the people You have put in my life:
both for those you have given me to love,
and for those who love me;
for Your miracles;
for holding me up and never letting go;
for all Your gifts to me;
for seeing, hearing, touching;
for laughter, for tears;
for the ability to feel;
for the gift of life;
for the wonder and variety of Your creatures here on earth;
for the mystery of Your presence and Your glory;
for the promise of eternally living with You.
Thank You, Lord.

CHAPTER FOURTEEN

OUR FOCUS SHOULD BE ON LOVING OTHERS:

JESUS IS OUR EXAMPLE - SERVE OTHERS

"Who, being in very nature God, did not consider equality with God something to be used to his own advantage; rather, he made himself nothing by taking the very nature of a servant, being made in human likeness. And being found in appearance as a man, he humbled himself by becoming obedient to death— even death on a cross." (Philippians 2:6-8)

A few years ago I was living in the city of Baltimore. My husband Daniel was pastoring a church there. One morning I was driving up a busy street in our neighborhood when I saw a man lying comatose outside a tavern. The paramedic had just arrived and was stooped down beside him, while a city ambulance waited nearby. *I thought to myself: how often have I seen that, someone drunk or high on drugs, and the city police and ambulance arrive and rescue the person, only to see him or her on the streets again soon thereafter, in the same state as before. And I thought:*

How many of our tax dollars go to this seemingly useless endeavor to help people like this?

Immediately, the Lord spoke to me and said, *"I died for them, Kathy, just as much as I died for you.* **Every single person is important to me."**

I was chastised. I no more deserved His love than that drunken man did, and yet God loves us both unreservedly and completely. I am to love others, as He loves me. We are to act as Jesus would – we are His body here on earth.

What does God want, then? *First, to love Him above all else, and second, to love others as we love ourselves.*

"[Jesus] answered, 'Love the Lord your God with all your heart and with all your soul and with all your strength and with all your mind'; and, 'Love your neighbor as yourself.'" (Luke 10:27).

CHAPTER FIFTEEN

LIVE IN MY WORD, NOT YOUR FEELINGS

"All Scripture is given by inspiration of God and is profitable for doctrine, for reproof, for correction, for instruction in righteousness." (2 Tim. 3:16)

"The law of the LORD is perfect, refreshing the soul. The statutes of the LORD are trustworthy, making wise the simple." (Psalm 19:7)

Another wonderful example of God's instruction to me was some years back, when I was living in Virginia with my second husband, "Joe". I was feeling very discouraged and overwhelmed. My stepson was in a lot of trouble, doing drugs, stealing things and hanging out with generally bad company. As I headed into work, I worried about my husband and my stepson, angry with both myself and them, and completely depressed. God spoke to me. He said, ***"Live in My Word, not your feelings."***

What a change occurred in me when I heard these words! I was to rely on His promises, not my feelings. His Word told me to rejoice in Him, to offer Him a sacrifice of praise, *and to trust Him*. These verses came to mind:

"I can do all things through Christ who strengthens me" (Philippians 4:13);

"I have loved you with an everlasting love" (Jeremiah 31:3);

"[His] mercies are new every morning" (Lamentations 3:22);

"God is my refuge and strength, a very present help in times of trouble" (Psalm 46:1);

"The Lord shall preserve thee from all evil" (Psalm 121:7).

Think on these things.

I cannot trust my feelings – they run both hot and cold, as St. Paul says. I <u>can</u> trust God's Word, unchanging and always true. He speaks to us in Scripture. We need to soak ourselves in it, so that we are prepared when Satan attacks us, when he tempts us, and when he tries to deceive us.

Long ago, when Jesus was in the wilderness and tempted by Satan, He used Scripture for every reply to the devil's words. Let's follow our Lord's example!

Satan will try to twist God's Word, with half-truths, just as he did when the serpent slyly asked Eve in the garden, *"Did God really say you can't eat of every tree?"* (Genesis 3). Then Satan said, *"you shall not die if you eat of this tree"*, and Eve was deceived and ate of it. We know the end of that story!

Lean into Scripture. Study to know God's Word, and when the devil next tempts you, foil him with the promises and truths of Scripture. You are God's child now, and you are protected with the seal of the Holy Spirit! Jesus is by your side – turn and look at Him. Speak His truths to your soul.

*"But [Jesus] answered and said, 'It is written, 'Man shall not live on **bread alone**, but on every word that proceeds out of the mouth of God.'"* (Matthew 4:4)

CHAPTER SIXTEEN

DECEPTION:
BE WARY OF SATAN'S WILES

"Vice is a creature of such awful mien
That to be hated needs but to be seen.
But too oft seen, familiar with its face,
We first endure, then pity, then embrace."
(from "Essay on Man", Alexander Pope)

*R*ecently I watched on Netflix an episode from "Frasier" (the popular television series from the '90's), an episode I had seen already as a rerun on television the previous year. This particular show was about Frasier mistakenly being identified as a gay man, and the resulting comedic errors when a gay man Frasier admired thought Frasier was gay as well. The first time I had seen it I was dismayed by the cavalier acceptance of a perverse and sinful lifestyle, but as I watched it a second time, I found myself viewing it all much more lightly and laughing as well. It struck me how easily we will accept a vice that has become familiar to us, as the poet Alexander Pope wrote in his "Essay on Man" (quoted in the chapter heading above). How even with the best of intentions and with the knowledge that an action is wrong, we can get used to a sin and accept it, even approve it over time. We too readily allow ourselves to be drawn in by Satan's wiles, even to the point of embracing that which we initially knew was evil.

Sometimes we are just plainly deceived. There is no getting around it. Just as Eve was first deceived by Satan in the Garden and then drew Adam into sin as well, we find times when we believe something that is not true. We act in ways that in retrospect we realize were taking us down a disastrous path away from God.

When I was in my 20's, I had friends who were convinced they were gay and were "born that way". This puzzled me, but in my attempt to fit together two opposing viewpoints – i.e., God clearly telling us homosexual acts are wrong and my desire to see my friends happy, I rationalized that if a person was "born that way" and only felt an attraction to their same sex, then surely they must be allowed to love and to have a relationship the same as a heterosexual would. I even argued for accepting the homosexual's "right to love" if they were truly born that way. It wasn't until a few years later, when I came to know Jesus as a real Person and not just God somewhere up in heaven, that I was convicted by the Holy Spirit and realized my conceit (telling God that I knew better than He did!). I then said to God with newfound obedience and humility, "I don't understand why this is so, but I accept Your Word that homosexual behavior is wrong no matter what feelings people may have about it."

Once I had declared that obedience to God's Word was more important than my human understanding, the Lord did a marvelous thing. A friend invited me to a meeting of a group in New York City called L.I.F.E. ministries (Living in Freedom Eternally). At that gathering I heard several men and women talk about their life experiences, and how God brought them out of the homosexual lifestyle and healed them, emotionally and spiritually. Some were now happily married and with children. Most described a childhood with either sexual abuse, or early memories of being afraid of a violent and emotionally abusive parent. I then understood how a person may so turn away from their parent, even as an infant (a baby boy afraid of an alcoholic father, for instance), that even before any conscious decisions are made, that small boy rejects becoming like his feared father, for instance, and instead identifies strongly with his mother. For a girl, it is often sexual molestation at an early age that makes her fear all men.

These are just two examples. There are of course many more reasons why a person may end up feeling attracted only to someone of the same sex, or may be confused about their gender identity. An illustration that may be helpful is to understand that sexual feelings and desires are similar to a river with a strong current. If the natural course of that river is obstructed or dammed up, the current will find another direction to go.

After hearing these testimonies, I realized that a child's psyche could be so damaged at an early age that he or she growing up cannot remember a time when they felt differently, and so they believe themselves to be born that way. This belief that homosexuality is inborn is accepted by many in our culture today, but it is still a deception. There is no "gay gene". The good news, the most marvelous news, is that God did not make anyone to be homosexual. Instead, He offers healing and hope to anyone caught up in that compulsive behavior for whatever reason. It is also true that Scripture does say some are born eunuchs, and some make themselves eunuchs for the Kingdom of God. I.e., not everyone is designed to be married and to have a sexual relationship. God offers healing, however, for those who are confused about their sexual identity or caught up in unhealthy, sin-sick behaviors.

God's Word tells us that the only appropriate sexual union is within the covenanted marriage of a man and woman. No sexual relations outside of marriage are acceptable. He desires to heal each one of us of our emotional wounds and sin-sick areas in our minds and bodies and souls. There is hope for everyone caught up in addictions of any kind, including an addiction to sinful or perverse sexual behavior.

As Christians, we need to offer hope and healing for the person who is convinced he or she is born a homosexual. We should not accept the deception that our feelings are always right, as they sometimes come from early emotional wounds or a deceived place in our spirits. We are good at deceiving ourselves! I remember a country song I heard years ago, in which the man sang "this can't be wrong, because it feels so right", when he was singing about adultery. **It can be wrong even when it feels right!** We are sheep that easily go astray! This is why we must rely on God's Word for guidance, and not just our feelings.

Jesus wants to heal us and He is perfectly able to heal us in every respect, including all compulsive sins and addictions. But He will not force us to obey Him. We must be willing to obey His laws even if at times we don't fully understand why. Trust Him! He is our Creator. He knows what is best for us. He WANTS to help us! We only need to ask for His help. He DELIGHTS in helping us! We are His children. **He loves us!**

Let us choose life and truth. His Word is trustworthy and can be believed. Follow Him!

"All Scripture is God-breathed and is useful for teaching, rebuking, correcting and training in righteousness." (II Timothy 3:16)

CHAPTER SEVENTEEN

ALWAYS START
THE DAY WITH JESUS

"Your statutes are wonderful, therefore I obey them. The unfolding of your words gives light, it gives understanding to the simple." (Psalm 119:129-130).

There is nothing I can say to match the beautiful words above taken from the Psalms. His Word gives light; it gives understanding. When I start the day with Jesus, when I read Scripture and allow time for it to soak into my spirit, I am renewed and refreshed. It is as if my spirit has been given wings to fly to heaven and spend time with my Lord and Savior. I come away changed. My spirit is "light", my burdens lifted, my heart filled with joy.

There is no greater delight than simply sitting in the Lord's company and allowing Him to love you, and giving Him your love back. This is what my spirit longs for; this is what I was made for: to enjoy God and to praise Him forever. I pray that each of you reading this will come to that place, if you have not already, of delighting in Him alone.

I am aware that I do not always reach that place either, despite my having been refreshed at the well of "living waters" so many times. Sometimes I still forget to do this. I get distracted or drawn away. Or perhaps my heart is heavy or oppressed and I just do not allow God in, even if I read His Word and pray. Press in, friends! Recall the great things God has done for you, just as David does in the Psalms. *"Enter His gates with thanksgiving, and His courts with praise."* (Psalm 100:4).

A sacrifice of praise certainly means that sometimes we will not feel like thanking God for anything. We may be angry at Him, or holding a grudge in our hearts towards another, or just physically exhausted. But press in, my friends! Do not let discouragement or Satan's wiles turn you away from the One who lives within you by the power of the Holy Spirit, the One who calls you to Himself, and *"delights over you with singing."* (Zephaniah 3:17).

What happiness, what joy awaits us in heaven! And even now we can experience some of that joy. We NEED God. If I start my day with Him, things fall in place so naturally as I follow Him, and do what is in front of me to do for that day. My mind rests peacefully on Him. However, if I am anxious or worried, or allow something to make me angry, my peace is destroyed and I have left Jesus out. **Jesus never leaves us. But we can walk away from Him.** When this happens, return quickly to Him as soon as you recognize your laxity, and offer Him your praise.

If you are having trouble being thankful, start with the simplest things. Look up at the sky, at the sun or the stars. Look at all God has made of beauty on the earth, including yourself! For you are *"fearfully and wonderfully made"* (Psalm 139:14). Reading some of the Psalms has often helped me. For instance, David says: *"I call as my heart grows faint; lead me to the rock that is higher than I. For you have been my refuge, a strong tower against the foe."* (Psalm 61:2-3).

Finally, thank Him for the greatest gift of all – His Son dying in your place so that you can have eternal life with Him. No matter how hard it is for you now, no matter what your present circumstances, you <u>will</u> be with Him in glory, and enjoy perfect peace and happiness some day in the future, which is not far away at all in heavenly time. How He loves us! How He provides for us! Praise Him, praise Him, praise Him! Hallelujah, Hallelujah, Hallelujah! Thank you, Jesus! Thank you, Jesus!!

CHAPTER EIGHTEEN

I AM A UNIQUE PERSON AND HAVE A SPECIAL PURPOSE IN GOD'S PLAN FOR MY LIFE THAT ONLY I CAN FULFILL

"For I know the plans I have for you," declares the Lord, "plans to prosper you and not to harm you, plans to give you hope and a future." (Jeremiah 29:11)

God has given each of us particular gifts and talents to use to serve Him. God will always give us everything we need to fulfill His purpose in our lives. But we must respond with obedience to His will in order to see these plans brought to fruition. Sometimes we will not be able to see what His purposes are, but need to blindly follow Him as He lights only one step at a time (Psalm 119:105).

There have been times in my life when I knew that I had chosen the wrong path in disobedience. There are also times when I have not been sure what direction He wants me to go.

Even though I wanted to do His will, I was not sure what His will was for me at that time. Sometimes it is obvious; sometimes not. For instance, if we study God's Word we will know a lot about how He wants us to live in relationship to Him and to others (*see* the Ten Commandments). But we may need to wait patiently to hear God's voice about a particular decision regarding a career move or a marriage partner, or other life-changing matters.

Jesus was in perfect communion with God at all times, and so He always knew He was doing exactly what God wanted Him to do in every moment of His life here on earth. But every other human being that has ever lived goes off in his own direction sooner or later, sometimes to their own destruction. We can start with Adam and Eve, continue on with Cain, et cetera, et cetera.

Thankfully, the Bible does not hide the sins of even our greatest saints, so we can understand that God loves us "just as we are", with all our waywardness and blatant imperfections. **The truth is that we are all lost and need a Savior.** Therefore, God sent Jesus, His only begotten Son, to pay the penalty for our sins. He is the Lamb without blemish, whose blood makes atonement for our sins (*see* John 3:16). Praise God!

"Now we see through a glass darkly, but in heaven we will see Him face to face" (I Cor. 13:12). How do we live in this world and know His will? How do we walk with Him here and now and fulfill His purpose for our lives? I am very aware of my many failings and weaknesses and the countless times I did not do what I should have done, but this is what I have learned so far about finding God's will.

First, seek His face. Everything I am planning to do needs to be prayed about, and given over to God. When I wake up in the morning I must set aside time for God before anything else. Reading the Bible and praying are essential to my spirit, as well as being open to listening for His Spirit.

Second, live in the present. Follow God's leading, and do whatever He puts before you to do in that day. Listen for the Holy Spirit's promptings. Whatever work He has given you to do, do it to the best of your ability - whether it is mopping the kitchen floor or advising the President of the United States. If you are in a job that you do not like, do it well anyway, but pray and ask God to prepare you and to open the doors to work you love. Pursue the dreams diligently that God has put in your heart that line up with your talents, even if others dismiss you or belittle your dreams. Continue to seek His will and trust Him to prepare you for *"the good works that He wants you to walk in"* (Ephesians 2:10).

Be patient and persevere. Be prepared to be surprised. Be flexible. God may find it most important that even if you feel hurried, you stop to help the stranger at the supermarket, or that you take a walk with your child in the park and smell the flowers rather than wash the dishes. I cannot tell you what God has planned for you. The wonder of it is that each of us is uniquely made, and with a unique purpose that only God knows. *No one else knows you as He does.*

His desire is that You will go to Him and seek His face. He wants a relationship with you and will guide you. Read His Word, pray, surrender your will to Him. Trust Him. He will not give you a stone when you ask for bread. He knows all things and has designed all things according to His purposes. His Spirit working within you will give you direction, often in surprising and wonderful ways.

If He seems silent on a matter, be patient and wait for an answer. He loves you and will never forsake you. He is delighted to answer your needs. You will have tests and trials, but if you have given your life to Him, *He is with you always* and will guide you.

The things that are most important to God are not evident in the ways of the world. As the poem says, "getting and spending, we lay waste our powers." ("The world is too much with us" by Wordsworth). But God says: *"Seek ye first the kingdom of God, and all these things will be added unto you."* (Matthew 6:33).

Live every moment of the day in conversation with Jesus, as best as you are able. I have been trying to do this for some time, but I am so easily distracted. I know how difficult this is and seemingly impossible to ever accomplish. Nevertheless, I know that in conversing with Jesus I find the perfect peace and assurance that I seek, and the strength to walk with Him every moment of the day, and to do His will. Centuries ago, someone said that the *"prayer without ceasing"* that the Apostle Paul suggests should simply be: *"Lord, have mercy."* This prayer is a wonderful place to start. In my spirit I often just say, *"Jesus, help!"* (And He does.)

Of course, perfectly following His will won't happen fully until heaven, but in the present moment calling on Jesus is the answer to all our stress and anxiety. He will guide you in the path He has prepared for you. He promises a unique and fulfilling life in Him. He loves you!! He knows the completely unique work He has prepared for you to do. <u>There is no one like you</u>! Seek Him first. He will direct your path.

"I have come that they may have life, and that they may have it more abundantly." (John 10:10).

CHAPTER NINETEEN

THE KEY TO HAPPINESS IN THIS LIFE

"Now that I, your Lord and Teacher, have washed your feet, you also should wash one another's feet. I have set you an example that you should do as I have done for you." (John 13:14-15)

Surely one of the keys to true happiness is serving others and forgetting yourself. How many times do I have to learn this lesson? Jesus gives many examples in the Gospels, but perhaps the most famous and soul-stirring is the story of the foot-washing at the Last Supper. Jesus takes a towel and washbasin and washes the feet of <u>all</u> of his disciples, including Judas. No wonder His disciples were shocked at His actions. Jesus, the King of the Universe, stoops to wash the feet of those who, by all rights, should be serving Him! Surely one reason He does this is to show us how to live as a servant to others. We are to put the other person's needs first, even when it costs us.

This was brought home to me in a recent incident. I came home upset and angry with myself at not doing as well as I had hoped in my first time conducting a local flute choir. When tuning the choir (made up of all volunteer amateur flutists), I had difficulty getting them in tune, and I was unhappy with the rehearsal. I came home angry and focused only on my failure at not getting to the standard I had set for myself. Instead of thinking how I could serve them and help them enjoy making music together, I was seeing only my imperfections and perceived failure. I lost the joy of serving them and all of us having fun doing it by focusing only on my own imperfections.

Have you found yourself grousing and complaining about some small thing, and suddenly something happens where your attention is diverted and you must help someone? For instance, while I was riding the bus in New York City, someone got on who was having difficulty walking even with a cane. I got up from my front seat and moved to the back so that that person could sit down. I felt good that I was able to help someone by even this small act of kindness, which cost me nothing. Or perhaps a friend calls in crisis and needs to talk, and I must stop what I am doing, even if I dislike the interruption, in order to give her my full attention. I am glad afterwards that I was able to be of help, even if only to listen.

Jesus often turns our priorities upside down. There were nine-ty-nine safe in the fold, but it is the one lost sheep that He went out to find.

Please don't misunderstand me. It is fine and natural to be happy and to feel good about ourselves when we accomplish a major goal – whether it is passing that final exam or scoring the winning run in a baseball game. God is pleased with our accomplishments and rejoices with us. But I wonder if it doesn't please Him even more, and He smiles lovingly at us, when we do some small act of kindness in service to others, perhaps the one unnoticed by anyone else.

Will I remember more the child's delight when I pushed her on the swing, higher and higher, or when I played my debut concert at Carnegie Recital Hall? I am not sure, but perhaps the former is more important than the latter in God's scheme of things. At the very least, both are significant.

Oh, what a God we have!! What an amazing thing, that He came to serve us, that He *"emptied himself"* for our sakes (Phil. 2). His delight is in helping <u>us</u>, when He has every right to ask for our worship and obeisance, as our Lord and our King.

Can you imagine appearing before an earthly king or queen--Queen Elizabeth of England for instance, and when you go to bow down she takes your hand, stops you, and instead bows to you? How would you feel? Honored? Shocked? Speechless? When Jesus stooped and washed their feet, how do you suppose the disciples felt?

We are loved far more than we can begin to imagine! See how Jesus bends low to help us, as He wipes the tears from our eyes and comforts us, even in those situations where we have brought calamity upon ourselves. There is no name-calling, no grudge held, no accusations.

Instead He says, *"Come, child. Come into my arms and receive my tender words of love."*

"Come, child. Come to Me. I love you."

"Therefore, there is now no condemnation for those who are in Christ Jesus" (Romans 8:1)

CHAPTER TWENTY

IF GOD IS IN CONTROL, WHY DO BAD THINGS HAPPEN?

"And the God of peace will crush Satan under your feet shortly."
(Romans 16:20)

"And the devil who had deceived them was cast into the lake of fire and brimstone, where the beast and the false prophet are; and they shall be tormented day and night forever and ever."
(Revelation 20:10)

"$\mathcal{B}$ut," you may ask, "how about the bad things that happen? How can this be a good God, if He is in complete control and yet allows horrific evils to occur?"

I do not have a complete answer for you. This is not something we can understand from our perspective here on earth. Some things are a mystery to us and we will not understand them fully until we are in heaven. As I Cor. 13:12 says: *"For now we see through a glass darkly; but then face to face."* (KJV)

If you say that is a cop-out, I agree. But we are God's **created beings**, we are **not** God. We cannot **be** God, nor understand His ways. As Isaiah says: *"For my thoughts are not your thoughts, neither are your ways my ways,"* declares the Lord. *"As the heavens are* *higher than the earth, so are my ways higher than your ways and my thoughts than your thoughts."* (Isaiah 55:8-9)

However, we can understand from studying Scripture many things, and God reveals to us through the Holy Spirit many things. **We can be sure of His love. We can be sure of our salvation through Christ's sacrifice. We can be sure that His promises are true.** When He tells us that one day Satan will be bound in the lake of fire, and that we will live in perfect peace in heaven without any tears, with the lion and the lamb lying down together, we can know that **evil is limited and will cease, whereas God is unlimited and will never cease.**

We are promised that although there is suffering now, these will have an end. Even God's own son, Jesus, was not spared suffering. In fact, the most terrible suffering imaginable: He was betrayed and abandoned by His friends, beaten and hung to die on the cross. He was spit on and cursed, when He was *without* sin and deserved none of these things. He did this for *us*. He paid the full price for *our* sins.

As Dietrich Bonhoeffer said in his book *"The Cost of Discipleship"*: we are not saved by cheap grace but at a very high cost. *Jesus paid the price for us because of His love for us.* I can never doubt His love! He has shown me His love in countless ways throughout my life as I walk with Him. If you look back over your life, you can surely see His guiding hand as well. Most of all, He has shown us His love through the death of Jesus on the cross, who died in our place and took the punishment for our sins, so that we could live with Him forever (*See* John 3:16).

We can know His love by the power of the Holy Spirit dwelling within our spirit, even when there are times in our emotions we cannot "feel" it. We walk by faith and not by sight here on this earth. That does not make the experience less real. We are spiritual beings, not merely physical, and in that sense our spirits are more real than our physical bodies, since our spirit lives forever, while the physical body decays and wastes away.

The fact that you are living and breathing and under-standing this as you read should be sufficient proof of God's love for you, for He made you and gave you life! Your life is not your own; you did not give yourself the breath of life--God did. All that you have here, all that you experience of good-ness and beauty in this world, is not of your own making, but is His gift to you! **He created you to know Him, to love Him, and to enjoy Him forever. He longs for you to know Him.**

His Holy Spirit speaks to you in your heart. You know in your spirit that He is calling to you. He has placed that longing in your heart to know Him, and nothing else will fully satisfy you until you come to Him and receive Him. His love is so complete, beyond all earthly love. (*"I have loved you with an everlasting love; I have drawn you with unfailing kindness."* Jeremiah 31:3).

We can trust God's Word. When He says *"all things work together for good for those who love God and are called according to His purpose"* (Romans 8:28), we can test that promise in our own lives and see that it is true.

Even my worst loss, my worst suffering--losing my daugh-ters--has been used for good in my life, both in ways I know and probably also in ways I don't know. Most importantly, I found Jesus' love and the assurance of heaven as a result of these expe-riences. **Would I have known the depth of God's love without going through those things?** I don't know. I only know that what God allowed to be taken away from me for reasons He alone knows--that the losses I have suffered, as deep as they are--cannot be compared with what I have gained in knowing Jesus and the depths of His love. Therefore I am satisfied in His love, and I can say with certainty that *He has used every pain, every sorrow in my life for good,* as strange as that may sound to someone who does not yet know God, nor met Jesus.

Walk in faith. Each of us has a unique path and a unique purpose. God refines us with fire, but we will not be burned up. He will bring you through a brighter gem for Him to reflect His glory in your life. *"See, I have refined you, though not as silver; I have tested you in the furnace of affliction."* (Isaiah 48:10.)

If you still wonder if God is omnipotent, here are some beautiful Scripture verses to read and ponder (there are countless verses on God's omnipotence in the Bible – this is just one place of many):

From Job 38:

Then the LORD *spoke to Job out of the storm. He said:*

²"Who is this that obscures my plans with words without knowledge?
³ Brace yourself like a man; I will question you, and you shall answer me.
⁴ "Where were you when I laid the earth's foundation? Tell me, if you understand.
⁵ Who marked off its dimensions? Surely you know! Who stretched a measuring line across it?
⁶ On what were its footings set, or who laid its cornerstone—
⁷ while the morning stars sang together and all the angels shouted for joy?

⁸ "Who shut up the sea behind doors when it burst forth from the womb,
⁹ when I made the clouds its garment and wrapped it in thick darkness,
¹⁰ when I fixed limits for it and set its doors and bars in place,
¹¹ when I said, 'This far you may come and no farther; here is where your proud waves halt'?

¹² "Have you ever given orders to the morning, or shown the dawn its place,
¹³ that it might take the earth by the edges and shake the wicked out of it?
¹⁴ The earth takes shape like clay under a seal; its features stand out like those of a garment.
¹⁵ The wicked are denied their light, and their upraised arm is broken.

^{16} *"Have you journeyed to the springs of the sea or walked in the recesses of the deep?*
^{17} *Have the gates of death been shown to you? Have you seen the gates of the deepest darkness?*
^{18} *Have you comprehended the vast expanses of the earth? Tell me, if you know all this.*

^{19} *"What is the way to the abode of light? And where does darkness reside?*
^{20} *Can you take them to their places? Do you know the paths to their dwellings?*
^{21} *Surely you know, for you were already born! You have lived so many years!*
^{22} *"Have you entered the storehouses of the snow or seen the storehouses of the hail,*
^{23} *which I reserve for times of trouble, for days of war and battle?*

^{24} *What is the way to the place where the lightning is dispersed, or the place where the east winds are scattered over the earth?*
^{25} *Who cuts a channel for the torrents of rain, and a path for the thunderstorm,*
^{26} *to water a land where no one lives, an uninhabited desert,*
^{27} *to satisfy a desolate wasteland and make it sprout with grass?*

^{28} *Does the rain have a father? Who fathers the drops of dew?*
^{29} *From whose womb comes the ice? Who gives birth to the frost from the heavens*
^{30} *when the waters become hard as stone, when the surface of the deep is frozen?*

^{31} *"Can you bind the chains of the Pleiades? Can you loosen Orion's belt?*
^{32} *Can you bring forth the constellations in their seasons or lead out the Bear with its cubs?*

³³ Do you know the laws of the heavens? Can you set up God's dominion over the earth?

³⁴ "Can you raise your voice to the clouds and cover yourself with a flood of water?
³⁵ Do you send the lightning bolts on their way? Do they report to you, 'Here we are'?
³⁶ Who gives the ibis wisdom or gives the rooster understanding?
³⁷ Who has the wisdom to count the clouds? Who can tip over the water jars of the heavens
³⁸ when the dust becomes hard and the clods of earth stick together?

³⁹ "Do you hunt the prey for the lioness and satisfy the hunger of the lions
⁴⁰ when they crouch in their dens or lie in wait in a thicket?
⁴¹ Who provides food for the raven when its young cry out to God and wander about for lack of food?.....

And from Job 42:1 ,5-6 (King James version):

"Then Job answered the Lord and said, "I know that thou canst do everything, and that no thought can be withholden from thee... I have heard of thee by the hearing of the ear, but now mine eye seeth thee, wherefore I abhor myself, and repent in dust and ashes."

CHAPTER TWENTY-ONE

THERE IS A HEAVEN!

(And If We Have Accepted Jesus As Our Savior, We Will Go To Heaven When We Die.)

"Men of Galilee," they said, "why do you stand here looking into the sky? This same Jesus, who has been taken from you into heaven, will come back in the same way you have seen him go into heaven." (Acts 1:11).

"But our citizenship is in heaven. And we eagerly await a Savior from there, the Lord Jesus Christ". (Philippians 3:20)

We can trust God's perfect plan for our lives. As believers, our purposes and our life's work are in His hands. I will miss my daughters for the rest of the days of my life here on earth, but I know I will see them again in heaven, and what an amazing reunion that will be!!

There have been several stories passed down in my family about those times when the veil between heaven and earth seems almost rent in two, and we get a brief glance of the incredible beauty and glory that awaits us. These incidents usually relate to times when those we love are facing death. My maternal grandmother,

Clara Bankson Hastings, died at age sixty of leukemia, when my mother was only nineteen. Since I never knew my grandmother, Mom would often tell me about her life. When my grandmother was dying, Mom told me that Clara looked up and said joyfully, "Why, mother, why, Rose!," just as if she were greeting them after an absence (her mother and sister had both died before her).

When my older brother Doug had a severe stroke a few years ago and was in the hospital, he told me that he saw Jesus standing on a hill, and as my brother approached him, Jesus told him to go back, that it wasn't his time yet. My brother fully recovered and lived five more years before he passed away. My sister Sue's husband also died a few years ago, and she speaks of a vision in which she saw him smiling and wearing a white robe in heaven, along with many other experiences.

There are several books written in recent years about the experiences of people who describe going briefly to heaven and coming back. There is much to sort out and it can be very confusing about what is real and what may be simply someone's wishful thinking or desire for fame.

Our best source is always the Scriptures and what God reveals to us of heaven in His Word. Sometimes God gives us signs or glimpses of the joy and peace in Heaven as well, and this can comfort and encourage us. One year, on the twenty-third birthday of my first daughter, Mary Rose, I was walking to my workplace in Washington, D.C, and sadly wondered if anyone else remembered her birthday. I did not even know if my ex-husband, her father, would remember that this was the birthday of his first daughter, since he had remarried and had had other children, and we had not been in contact in many years.

Mary Rose had died at age two months, having never left the hospital where she was born, and none of my family had ever gotten to meet her. No one had called me that morning before I left for work, and I wondered if any of my family even remembered what this date meant. As I thought about this day, her 23rd

earthly birthday, I said to myself, "*Is there anyone besides me that this day is important to, who even cares?*"

Suddenly there was a picture in my head of a young woman, standing with arms akimbo, in a lovely aproned knee-length full-skirted dress. With some force and almost indignantly she said, "*It matters to me!*"

I was so startled. It was as if I had a quick glimpse of the young lady that Mary Rose had become, growing up in heaven. I felt certain that it was she, telling me herself how glad she was to have been born, and making sure I knew that! It shook me out of my self-pity and I walked on to work, in awe that I was allowed this momentary view of my daughter and her personality. I treasure this memory today, and it has given me so much pleasure and joy over the years. You see, Mary Rose was unconscious and on a respirator for all but the first few days of her short life here on earth, and so I never got to know her personality here. What a gift to have this glimpse! And what an amazingly happy day that will be when I meet her again in heaven. I will never forget hearing her voice that day, and how she said, "*It matters to me!*"

God has His plans for you and they are good. He promises us that life in heaven will be perfect – literally perfect. It is sometimes hard to imagine what this could be like, since all we know here is a fallen, sinful world. We have wonderful earthly experiences too, and most of us know, if we have been fortunate, what it is like to love and be loved here on earth. But surely our experiences here will pale in comparison to the complete love and joy we will feel in heaven. But we are given "windows" to heaven sometimes, when we have a brief sense of the joy to come.

What have I learned from these experiences of loved ones passing on? First, be grateful for this moment now; live fully in the present. We only have the present – God alone knows the future. Second, you can trust God completely in everything. He will work out everything for good, even though you may not ever understand His ways until you get to heaven. Third, rejoice in the knowledge that He has promised you eternal life, and that this earthly life is not all there is. Finally, and most important: all of your life, including your salvation, is God's perfect gift to you, given through the costly grace of His Son's death on the cross, dying in your place to give you of His life. Be thankful!

"For God so loved the world, that He gave His only begotten Son, that whosoever believeth in Him should not perish, but have everlasting life." (John 3:16).(King James Version)

"When we all get to heaven, what a day of rejoicing that will be! When we all see Jesus, we'll sing and shout the victory!" (Hymn by Eliza E. Hewitt).

CONCLUSION

HIS LOVE TRANSFORMS ME

"But we all, with unveiled face, beholding as in a mirror the glory of the Lord, are being transformed into the same image from glory to glory, just as by the Spirit of the Lord." (II Corinthians 3:18)

As I write this, I am painfully aware of how far short I fall in the practice of my faith compared to my knowledge of what God wants me to do. I see that I have promised to love my husband, and yet I get angry at him for not living up to my standards, when I can't even live up to them myself! As Jesus' parable describes: why do I try to take the "speck of sawdust" out of my brother's eye, when I have a plank obstructing the vision in my own! (Luke 6:42).

I am selfish, self-absorbed, inconsiderate of others, impatient if anyone interrupts my plans, seeking my own pleasures, only momentarily moved to help another, quick to envy....I could go on and on, unfortunately. Yet Jesus looks at me and loves me. He knows the depths of my selfishness. But He also sees me as what He created me to be in His perfection, not the sad filthy rags I wear of my own making. He lifts me up out of the pit. He picks me up over and over again! It doesn't seem to matter how many times I fall into the dirt, He is always eager to pick me up, embrace me and wrap His loving arms around me. He always cleans me off and wraps me in a new white robe. His presence changes me. His Spirit softens my heart. His love transforms me!

Have you experienced this, my friend? Have you seen your own black heart, and been in wonder how God can love you so? I have and it is so. He loves us *no matter what.* He knows we cannot fix ourselves. He knows we are weak and lost creatures, like the sheep that has wandered away from the Shepherd. He does not wait for us to come back to the fold--*He knows we can't find the way!* He hunts us down. He is the Good Shepherd who searches us out and brings us back into His loving embrace.

The poem *"The Hound of Heaven"* by Francis Thompson speaks of this so beautifully. It has long been a favorite of mine. Here it is in part below: my final gift to you as I close this book. I hope that these reflections on my experiences of God's amazing love and power at work in my life will help build up your faith, and encourage you in your own walk with Him. **May God bless you, my friend!**

****

The Hound of Heaven
by Francis Thompson (1859-1907)

I fled Him, down the nights and down the days;
I fled Him, down the arches of the years;
I fled Him, down the labyrinthine ways
Of my own mind; and in the mist of tears
I hid from Him, and under running laughter.
Up vistaed hopes I sped;
And shot, precipitated,
Adown Titanic glooms of chasmed fears,
From those strong Feet that followed, followed after.
But with unhurrying chase,
And unperturbèd pace,

Deliberate speed, majestic instancy,
They beat--and a Voice beat
More instant than the Feet--
"All things betray thee, who betrayest Me."

I pleaded, outlaw-wise,
By many a hearted casement, curtained red,
Trellised with intertwining charities
(For, though I knew His love Who followed,
Yet was I sore adread
Lest having Him, I must have naught beside);
But if one little casement parted wide,
The gust of His approach would clash it to.
Fear wist not to evade, as Love wist to pursue.
Across the margent of the world I fled,
And troubled the gold gateways of the stars,
Smiting for shelter on their clanged bars;
Fretted to dulcet jars
And silvern chatter the pale ports o' the moon.
I said to dawn, Be sudden; to eve, Be soon;
With thy young skyey blossoms heap me over
From this tremendous Lover!
Float thy vague veil about me, lest He see!
I tempted all His servitors, but to find
My own betrayal in their constancy,
In faith to Him their fickleness to me,
Their traitorous trueness, and their loyal deceit.
To all swift things for swiftness did I sue;
Clung to the whistling mane of every wind.
But whether they swept, smoothly fleet,
The long savannahs of the blue;
Or whether, Thunder-driven,
They clanged his chariot 'thwart a heaven
Plashy with flying lightnings round the spurn o' their feet--
Still with unhurrying chase,

And unperturbèd pace,
Deliberate speed, majestic instancy,
Came on the following Feet,
And a Voice above their beat--
"Naught shelters thee, who wilt not shelter Me."

[some lines omitted here]

I stand amid the dust o' the mounded years--
My mangled youth lies dead beneath the heap.
My days have crackled and gone up in smoke,
Have puffed and burst as sun-starts on a stream.
Yea, faileth now even dream
The dreamer, and the lute the lutanist;
Even the linked fantasies, in whose blossomy twist
I swung the earth a trinket at my wrist,
Are yielding; cords of all too weak account
For earth with heavy griefs so overplussed.

[some lines omitted here]

Now of that long pursuit
Comes on at hand the bruit;
That Voice is round me like a bursting sea:
"And is thy earth so marred,
Shattered in shard on shard?
Lo, all things fly thee, for thou fliest Me!
Strange, piteous, futile thing,
Wherefore should any set thee love apart?
Seeing none but I makes much of naught," He said,
"And human love needs human meriting,
How hast thou merited--
Of all man's clotted clay the dingiest clot?
Alack, thou knowest not
How little worthy of any love thou art!

Whom wilt thou find to love ignoble thee
Save Me, save only Me?
All which I took from thee I did but take,
Not for thy harms.
But just that thou might'st seek it in my arms.
All which thy child's mistake
Fancies as lost, I have stored for thee at home;
Rise, clasp My hand, and come!"

Halts by me that footfall;
Is my gloom, after all,
Shade of His hand, outstreched caressingly?
"Ah, fondest, blindest, weakest,
I am He Whom thou seekest!
Thou dravest love from thee, who dravest Me."

****

POSTSCRIPT:
A LOVE LETTER TO JESUS

I love you, Jesus! You are my all in all. You are AMAZING! So kind and so gracious. Incredible love and peace fill my heart with Your presence. You ARE Love and Peace! *There is nothing to fear because You are with me.* You have held me in Your arms from the beginning, and I know at the end of my earthly life You will be holding me in Your arms.

How can I thank You enough? You gave up everything for me: your life in heaven, your power, complete peace and ecstasy, to come down and to be bound in a small human form, subject to all the evil Satan could manage to throw against You. You took the weight of all my sins upon Your back. You endured the most horrible suffering for my sake. It cost You everything, but You willingly stayed on the Cross so that I could be redeemed, and live with You forever. **What wondrous love is this!**

I owe You my life. I GIVE You my life. I surrender my life to You, to mold me as the potter molds the clay in his hands. Let me be still, and rest in Your arms.

Please use me, Lord, to reach others with Your love. Forgive me my sins, my utter selfishness. Help me look outward, and see others' needs. Help me to love others, while loving myself too. Thank you for each one You have put in my life. Bless them, and bless the readers of this book.

Blessed be the Lamb, who deserves all honor and glory and praise FOREVER AND EVER!

Thank You, Jesus.

****